The F.....

Las Vegas

The Family Fun Guide to Las Vegas

The Best Hotels, Attractions, Side Trips, and More

REVISED AND UPDATED

Connie Emerson

CITADEL PRESS
Kensington Publishing
www.kensingtonbooks.com

CITADEL PRESS BOOKS are published by

Kensington Publishing Corp.
850 Third Avenue
New York, NY 10022

All Kensington titles, imprints, and distributed lines are available at special quantity discounts for bulk purchases for sales promotions, premiums, fund-raising, educational, or institutional use. Special book excerpts or customized printings can also be created to fit specific needs. For details, write or phone the office of the Kensington special sales manager: Kensington Publishing Corp., 850 Third Avenue, New York, NY 10022, attn: Special Sales Department, phone 1-800-221-2647.

First printing: February 2002

10 9 8 7 6 5 4 3 2 1

Printed in the United States of America

Library of Congress Control Number: 2001094202

ISBN 0-8065-2239-9

Contents

You've been to Disneyland, Disney World, Six Flags, Over Almost Everywhere. You're looking for some-place different where everyone can have a great time—including the adults. The new family-oriented Las Vegas may well be your answer.

Every family needs one, and it's best when every family member has a say. How will you get there? What's the best length of time to stay? Who wants to go where? Thoroughly exploring the entertainment possibilities and discussing your expectations ahead of time will give you greater assurance that they'll be fulfilled.

Just as families come in all shapes and sizes, so do hotel and motel rooms. From penthouse suites in high-rise hotels to mom-and-pop motels, from RV parks to houseboats, this chapter explores lodging possibilities in and around the World's Entertainment Capital.

3. Feeding Time   35

It usually is a challenge trying to satisfy everyone's tastes. But Las Vegas—due to its enormous volume of tourists—has a greater variety of restaurants, cafes, and other eating places than any other city of its size in the world. That just about guarantees that whatever palate-pleasers you're looking for, you'll find them here.

4. Transportation Tips   57

Las Vegas is the fastest growing city in America, spreading out farther every day. But don't worry about logistics. This chapter tells you the best ways to get to wherever you're going.

5. Shopping Sprees   67

Looking for a glass clown made in Venice? A drum from Southwest Africa? Or a fistful of made-in-the-U.S.A. poker chips for your family room? Whether your shopping list includes designer gowns or buckskin leggings, original art or old movie posters, there's a place to buy whatever you're yearning for in Las Vegas—including nontacky souvenirs.

6. Attractions and Events   83

Theme parks with scary rides . . . Discovery museums . . . Battles between pirates and the British Navy . . . Theater productions especially for children: Las Vegas glitz and glitter combine with a wealth of organization and city-sponsored activities and special events to insure that there is something to do every minute of every vacation day.

Active families don't slow down just because they're on vacation. Golf, tennis, and other sports become even more important when they have extra time for them. This chapter tells you where to play your favorite games and about some new games you may not have played before.

True, lots of Las Vegas nighttime entertainment is of the adults-only variety. But there are just as many—or more—family-oriented things to do. Whether your family prefers nationally sanctioned auto races or ballet, country music and rodeo action or opera, you'll be pleased with the city's offerings of evening events.

Not all Las Vegas showroom offerings are appropriate for family viewing. In fact, minors aren't admitted to some of the productions. This chapter spotlights the shows that everyone will enjoy. It also includes tips on selecting the seats in your price range.

Not only are there lots of things to look at in Nevada's largest city, just drive an hour or less in almost any direction and you'll find more. Add a couple more hours and you can fly over the Grand Canyon or day trip to Zion National Park in Utah. Discover what to see outside Las Vegas.

The more you can find out about a place in advance of your visit, the better your chance of having a wonderful

time. This chapter tells you where to find out all you
need to know.

Acknowledgments

Every guidebook writer needs a lot of advice, since one person simply can't know everything about a place no matter how long he has lived there or how often she has visited. Inside sources are especially important for a family guide. Therefore, my thanks to the Las Vegas schoolteachers and parents who offered tips and information. Thanks, too, to the Las Vegas youngsters—and kids visiting the city with their parents—who told me what was cool and what definitely was not. A special thanks to the late Ken Evans, Keoki Hiaukulani, Roger Letourneau, Jenn Michaels, Don Payne, and Barbara Scully; to my editor, Michael Lewis; and to all the people who helped make the book a reality. And finally, thanks to my family—the two Ralphs, George, Taylor, and Kyle— for their love and support.

Introduction

"Family fun" is usually a euphemism for doing what the kids want, with an occasional time-out for parents. But in Las Vegas, with its abundance of attractions that appeal to people of all ages, no one has to feel like a martyr. Everyone can have a great time.

Granted, it wasn't always that way. Until the 1990s Las Vegas was known as Sin City, Sun City, America's Number One Adult Vacation Destination, and Disneyland for the Over-Twenty-One Crowd, but it was never known as a place for families to hang out together. Except for the midway attractions at Circus Circus, there wasn't a whole lot for youngsters and teenage tourists to do.

Then casino moguls decided that they were missing a bet by not going after the family trade—developing attractions that would keep the kids happy; especially those kids with one non-gambling parent and another who liked to spend some time at the tables or slot machines. They incorporated theme park features into their new hotel/casinos with hopes that conventioneers and people attending trade shows would bring their families with them; that Mom, Dad, and the youngsters would choose Las Vegas as the year's vacation spot instead of Disney World or Waikiki.

The results of this strategy have not been as economically impressive as when rooms are occupied solely by adults (minors are prohibited by law from gambling so per-room occupant spending is lower). These days, although the advertising is back again on adult entertainment, the family-orientation trend has provided a host of new attractions calculated to captivate the younger generation. Whether the city's promoters like it or not, Las Vegas has become a family vacation destination.

The tourist count has gone up. Las Vegas is now the country's top vacation spot. More than thirty-six million visitors came to play or conduct business in Nevada's largest city during 2001, and those numbers are expected to keep climbing.

It's a far cry from Las Vegas in its early days. Although the Mormons sent a mission of thirty men to the area in the early 1850s to establish a fort and teach agriculture to the Indians, it wasn't until Las Vegas was designated a major division point by the Union Pacific Railroad in 1905 that the town was incorporated.

Even with the construction of nearby Hoover Dam in the early 1930s, Las Vegas remained a small town. After all, it was a hot and dusty place, smack in the middle of a desert where temperatures rise to 115 degrees Fahrenheit and higher in the summertime. Although gambling had been legalized in Nevada by an act of the state legislature in 1931, there were only a few gambling clubs in the downtown area and along the two-lane highway to Los Angeles.

Air conditioning, irrigation, and the post–World War II proliferation of casinos changed everything. On Christmas Day, 1946, Bugsy Siegel opened his celebrated Flamingo Hotel/Casino on what would later be known as the Strip, and Las Vegas was on its way to becoming "The Entertainment Capital of the World."

Some fifty-five years later, Las Vegas is a city of superlatives. Lavish hotel/casinos, robed in neon tubing and flashing lights, line the three-and-a-half-mile-long Strip. Downtown in Glitter

Gulch are a dozen and a half more, with an ever-increasing number of hotel/casinos going up in outlying areas.

Of the twenty largest hotels in the world, eighteen are in Las Vegas. And while Las Vegas is the thirty-second largest city in the United States, its airport, McCarran International, is the thirteenth busiest. The largest city in the United States established in the twentieth century, it's growing at a rate faster than any other metropolitan area in the country.

The city boasts more than three dozen golf courses, hundreds of restaurants, and shopping centers galore, including one with talking statues. It's a two-faced town. One face is layered with facades and fantasy, the other is much like that of any other city in the country with churches, parks, museums, and schools.

Because of the city's phenomenal growth, these are ever-changing faces. Older casinos are imploded or demolished by the wrecking ball to make room for larger, more impressive gambling palaces. The flags of dozens of new subdivisions wave in the desert breeze. In fact, so many area changes are taking place that for the past few years the telephone directory has been published every six months to keep pace.

One of the reasons for Las Vegas's huge number of tourists is that it's so easy to get to. Located in a broad valley with lots of growing room left, the area is well connected to other parts of the West. The major automobile route is I-15, which goes south to Los Angeles and north to Salt Lake City. U.S. 95 links Las Vegas to Reno in the north and Phoenix in the south. In addition, the city is served by Amtrak, bus lines, and eight hundred airplane flights a day.

Though Las Vegas is not a difficult city to get to know, choosing among its more than 120,000 guest rooms, hundreds of restaurants, and myriad entertainment possibilities can be confusing. Which brings us to the purpose of this book—showing you how to make the most of your family's Las Vegas vacation.

Each of the book's eleven chapters deals with a component

that can make or break a family holiday—accommodations, dining, sightseeing, or shopping. And since vacation budgets vary so widely, we explore both luxury and bare-bones lodgings, freebie pleasures and pricey treats, discount outlets and upscale boutiques, along with goods and services in the mid-price range.

We realize, too, that families come in all shapes and sizes; they're not all of the two-parents, one-child, or two-children variety. Therefore, families in this book can be interpreted to mean a single dad with his boys; a mother and her companion with their combined brood; grandparents and grandkids; blended families; or extended families—as long as one member of the group is a child or teenager.

So, read those parts of the book that are in sync with your particular family and its preferences, skip over those that aren't. Just remember that there's no "right" or "wrong" travel style, and that the essence of a perfect holiday is to go home with everyone saying "That was the best vacation ever."

A note on kids in casinos: While Nevada law prohibits anyone under age twenty-one from "loitering" where gambling is taking place, there's nothing wrong with passing through and checking out the sights and sounds.

CHAPTER 1

Vacation Plan

Most of us have experienced at least one trip that didn't turn out the way we had planned, precisely because we hadn't done enough planning. But that doesn't have to happen to you. You can avoid most of the common vacation pitfalls by researching the basic components of your trip two or three months—or even a year—in advance.

The first major decision is where to go. And this may not be as simple as it sounds—especially if you're considering Las Vegas. For Nevada's largest city is one of a kind.

It is a city of extremes—extreme heat in summer; an extremely high proportion of the world's largest hotels, accompanied by an enormous amount of glitz and glitter. There's a laissez faire attitude toward drinking, with alcoholic beverages served twenty-four hours a day—fine for people who don't have problems with alcohol abuse, but dangerous for those who do. Sex for sale is advertised on the streets and in the Yellow Pages (under "Escorts"). And many of the city's visitors seem to lose the inhibitions they have back home. Therefore, it's not an easy place for parents who want to keep their children unaware of those aspects of life.

Along with adult temptations, Las Vegas has an almost over-

1

whelming number of tempting things for children to do, including thrill rides such as roller coasters, arcades with games that are sometimes violent, and X-rated movies on hotel room television. Parents who are concerned about the safety of thrill rides, who abhor violent games, or who are concerned about their children's exposure to explicit sex may want to choose another holiday spot.

It's not the perfect destination, either, when adult family members have conflicting vacation expectations. For example, if one of the adults in your group is anticipating long hours at the video poker machines while the other looks after the kids, ask yourself some questions and answer them truthfully before you make your destination decision. Is the video poker player a good loser or does he or she get grumpy when money is lost? Does the significant other, who will be minding the children, love to spend great unrelieved gobs of time with them, or will she or he be resentful? Your answers may reveal that although Las Vegas could well be an ideal destination for the two of you as adults, it shouldn't be the one you choose for the family.

Otherwise, though, for families who want to take advantage of gaming's benefits (relatively low-room and -restaurant prices and an abundance of attractions, many of which are suitable for children) as well as the non-neon attractions in the city and surrounding area, Las Vegas can be a great place to vacation.

Because taking a family vacation requires more advance planning than a trip for one or two, once you've decided on Las Vegas as your destination, start planning!

Something as trivial (to grown-ups, anyway) as who sits where in the car or next to whom on the plane can become a major point of contention on a cross-country trip. But even before you've figured out the solutions to those kinds of problems, you'll have to decide whether you will travel to Las Vegas by plane or car, when you'll arrive, and how long you will stay.

Las Vegas is currently served by seventeen major North American airlines that fly regular schedules. They are:

Air Canada	800/776-3000
Alaska Airlines	800/426-0333
Allegiant Air	877/202-6444
America West	800/2-FLY-AWA
American Airlines	800/433-7300
Continental Airlines	800/525-0280
Delta Air Lines	800/221-1212
Frontier Airlines, Inc.	800/432-1359
Hawaiian Airlines	800/367-5320
Midwest Express	800/452-2022
National	888/757-5387
Northwest Airlines	800/225-2525
Southwest Airlines	800/435-9792
United Airlines	800/241-6522
United Express	800/453-9417
U.S. Airways	800/428-4322

If it can be arranged, everyone on the plane should have a window seat or at least a view for the landing at McCarran International Airport. For where else can you see an Egyptian pyramid and New York's skyscrapers practically across the street from each other?

The terminal itself is also like no other, with stylized metallic palm trees surrounding the slot machines, lots of bright lights, and popular showroom entertainers telling you via the sound system to "stay to your right and pass on the left" while you're on the moving sidewalks.

By Car

If you travel to Las Vegas by automobile, your arrival will be much less traumatic when you've acquired a map of the city beforehand (see chapter 11). Chances are, you'll enter the city either by U.S. 95, which runs more or less north and south through

Nevada; or U.S. 93, which connects Las Vegas with Phoenix; or Interstate 15, which goes between Los Angeles and Salt Lake City (and beyond).

To make driving life even easier, study the map before you leave home, tracing your route into the city and to your hotel or motel with a colored pencil or a highlighter. Time your arrival for before or after rush hour. If you don't, the whole family—and perhaps your car's radiator, too—will be steaming from the stop-start traffic around the Strip when you finally get to your hotel.

By Train

Because of a $9 million allocation in 1998, Amtrak service between Los Angeles and Las Vegas has been increased to seven round trips a day. Amtrack also provides a combination of railroad/bus service from various points including Chicago, Salt Lake City, and Phoenix.

Ticket Talk

Buying airline tickets for the family, especially if it's a large family, can be the single most expensive cost of your vacation. If you don't have deep pockets or scads of frequent flyer points, you'll probably be looking for the lowest possible fare.

By planning early, you can shop around for the best deals (or have a travel agent do it for you). You'll also be able to lock in seat assignments that please your family. Phone the airlines that serve the airports nearest you for the lowest available fares during the time you'll be vacationing, and ask specifically if they have any special fares for families traveling together.

You will find that airfares vary with the day of the week as well as the time of the year. This means that the more flexible you can be with your travel dates, the more likely you are to realize substantial savings.

In addition to telephoning the airlines' reservationists, watch the Sunday newspaper travel sections for ads. Bargain-fare advertisements may also appear midweek in newspapers such as the *Wall Street Journal* and major metropolitan dailies. Be aware, however, that most of the fabulously low-priced Las Vegas packages advertised in metropolitan newspaper travel sections—$235 for round-trip airfare from Minneapolis and three nights' stay at Treasure Island, for example—won't be for you unless everyone in your party is twenty-one years of age or over. Discounted tickets advertised by travel agencies, though they may have certain restrictions, can be used by anyone in your family and may, in fact, be cheaper than the children's rate.

If prices on two or more airlines are approximately the same, study the schedules to see which flights are nonstop or have the fewest stops and/or plane changes. Vacation time is often as valuable as money, and you don't want to spend any more of yours waiting in airports than is absolutely necessary.

Many of the airlines have begun serving prepackaged snacks in lieu of regular meals on their shorter flights. These mini-meals as a rule include foods kid like, such as fresh fruit, packaged cookies, power bars, bagels, and sandwiches. Airlines that serve regular meals usually offer special meals for children.

At least twenty-four hours before you leave, order any special meals your children might like. Simply call the reservations number of the airline on which you are ticketed. And to make the miles fly by more quickly, have each child carry a backpack filled with favorite toys, a Walkman or a CD player, books, and perhaps a snack or two.

By Bus

Although Greyhound buses also serve the city from various parts of the United States and Canada, there is very little bus travel to Las Vegas except from Los Angeles (about nineteen arrivals a day) and Phoenix (about six arrivals a day). There are two arrivals each day from Salt Lake City, but the trip takes about twice as long as it does by automobile. No buses run directly from Reno, 440 miles to the north. Instead, passengers are routed through California and must make two transfers; at Sacramento and at Los Angeles, resulting in a trip that takes nineteen hours.

If you drive, the amount of time you spend in Las Vegas can be somewhat flexible. When you're flying in and out, you have to determine your length of stay and its dates before you buy your tickets. A primary consideration may well be the tickets themselves. One common restriction on lower priced tickets is that the passengers who use them must stay over on a Saturday night. Since almost all Las Vegas accommodations cost more on weekend nights than they do on weekdays, however, you may be ahead buying higher priced tickets that don't have this restriction.

Other factors that enter in are time available and your family's staying power. Families with small children who haven't had much experience traveling together might decide that three days is sufficient. Others who like to explore any area they visit thoroughly may plan to stay a week. The average Las Vegas stay, incidentally, is approximately four days. In my opinion, that's just about right for the first-time visitor, because for many people it's an "I'm glad to have seen it, but once is enough" sort of place. Other first-timers, who decide Las Vegas is the most exciting place on the planet and feel their trips were too short, can begin planning their next trip on their way back home.

Accommodations

Arriving in Las Vegas without room reservations during the National Finals Rodeo (December), the huge Comdex convention (November), Consumer Electronics Show (January), or any other big event may mean you'll have to settle for less than desirable rooms or accommodations fifty miles away. At those times, you'll also find it virtually impossible to rent a car.

Over the past years, the Las Vegas Convention & Visitors Authority has attempted to mold the city into a destination with no seasonal highs and lows. And they have succeeded in making Las Vegas the country's number one convention site (each year, almost 4,000 conventions attract approximately 3,750,000 people and pump approximately $4 billion into the local economy). As a result, there's no real off-season, except for the period from mid-November through January (with the exception of National Finals Rodeo week and the days before and including New Year's).

At the busiest times of the year it's almost impossible to be assured of getting a room unless you book several months in advance. But the good news is that there are days of the week and times of the year when hotels and motels charge a good deal less for their rooms in order to maintain high occupancy levels.

When your vacation dates are cast in concrete and coincide with big events, you'll pay top dollar for your accommodations. If you have flexibility as to dates, those same rooms will probably cost you a lot less.

While dozens of companies in various parts of the country put together Las Vegas tours, these are almost always gambling junkets, and all participants must be over the age of twenty-one. Nongambling tours aren't usually suitable for families either, especially those with small children, since their itineraries are too adult oriented and are usually extremely structured. You may, however, be able to find airlines' accommodation packages that fit your requirements and save you money.

One word of advice: If you stay at one of the mega hotel/casinos, get a floor plan of the hotel for each person in your party who is old enough to read it. Also, upon arrival, stuff a picture postcard of the hotel in each child's backpack or pocket as insurance in case you should become separated. Even teenagers can forget the name of the place in which they're staying.

Analyzing the Attraction Options

After your transportation and accommodations have been decided upon, it's time to give some thought to what you all want to do while you're in Las Vegas. Explain the available options, then get input from everyone who is old enough to talk. You'll find information about attractions, activities, amusements, annual events, and nighttime entertainment by reading the chapters later in this book that are devoted to them.

To get supplemental information, such as that about exhibitions, performances, special events, and showroom entertainment that will take place while you're in town, write to the Las Vegas Convention & Visitors Authority (see chapter 11). The more specific your requests for information (e.g., recreational facilities, cultural performances, children's theater) the better your chances of finding out what you want.

Keep pen and paper handy while your family is discussing what each member would most like to do. Make a list of possible activities, attractions, and the like; then prioritize them according to the time available. Also include alternates in case first choices don't work out. For example, if you haven't realized before you get to Las Vegas that the Siegfried & Roy show costs $100.50 per person (that's $502.50 for a family of five!), you may decide to substitute some other evening entertainment.

When you're putting together your itinerary, remember that no one knows your family as well as the adults who are a part of it do. You're not your cousin Charley and his wife, or your neighbors down the block, so whatever they thought was great and however rigorous or laid back their schedules, such options may not work for you.

Use the knowledge you've gained through the years about your family and yourself. If Jason gets cranky when he hasn't had a chance to run off energy and Emily's a pill when she has to get up before nine, arrange your activities accordingly. If your spouse gets frantic if you don't have restaurant reservations by 4:00 P.M. and you're a disaster when the blood sugar gets low, take these factors into account while you're in the activity-planning process and everyone will have a much better time.

Packing Perspectives

Not many of us have packed the exactly right clothes for every trip we have taken. But whatever kind of clothing you pack for a Las Vegas vacation, you won't go too far wrong because it's an "anything goes" sort of place. Daytime apparel runs the fashion gamut from grunge to casual chic. At pricey restaurants and in the showrooms, you'll see people who are dressed to the nines in cocktail dresses and tuxedos; next to them, people wearing T-shirts and shorts. Most people, however, put on clothes that might be termed "dressy casual" when they go out for the evening. Although some of the better restaurants require that men wear sport coats, few of them require neckties. The children you see in these restaurants are usually dressed in party clothes, for after all, most kids consider dining out in style a special occasion.

There can be a problem, however, if you don't find out in advance what to expect as far as weather is concerned. I've seen planeloads of visitors from the northern United States shivering in their shirtsleeves when December temperatures dip and winds kick up the desert dust. They have arrived with the assumption that Las Vegas has a very warm climate. It does. But not necessarily in winter. While some days in November, December, and January are sunny and warm enough for shorts, on others you'll need a winter jacket and warm cap in order to be comfortable. And although April through October is virtually guaranteed to be shorts and sundress weather, you'll want to bring sweaters for protection *indoors* when air conditioning is turned up to the max.

Use the following temperature chart as a guideline for what to expect:

Month	Temperature Min. Max. (°F)		Humidity A.M. P.M. (%)		Average Rainfall (inches)
January	33	56	41	30	.50
February	37	67	36	26	.46
March	42	68	30	22	.41
April	49	77	22	15	.22
May	59	87	19	13	.22
June	68	98	15	10	.09
July	75	104	19	15	.45
August	73	110	14	18	.54
September	65	94	23	17	.32
October	53	81	25	19	.25
November	41	66	33	27	.43
December	33	57	41	33	.32

The most efficient clothes-packing technique is to put complete outfits for the children—underwear, shorts, top, and socks—in large plastic bags with zipper-type locks. Then just pull them out as needed.

Teenagers who pack their own bags are happier travelers than those whose parents decide which clothes they can bring along. The downside, of course, is that you may not much like what they've chosen to wear. But as one wise dad said, "I'd rather have strangers see them looking weird, than the people we know."

Time Out

There are times, even on vacation, when kids need a break from their parents. Unless your family includes teenagers who don't object too strenuously to looking after younger siblings, you'll need to make some decisions regarding child care.

Some people are too uncomfortable to have a good time if anyone but a family member or person well known to them is taking care of their children. They may decide to take the grandparents along or to bring their trusted sitter from home to Las Vegas with them. A second child care solution is to time your Las Vegas vacations so that friends with children will be on hand to trade off child-sitting responsibilities.

Another option is to use the licensed child care facilities provided by several casinos. Although MGM Grand is the only hotel on the Strip to have a licensed facility, an ever-increasing number of off-Strip casinos—including Boulder Station, Sunset Station, Sam's Town, Gold Coast, Suncoast, Orleans, and Santa Fe, have them. Most facilities take children from six months to twelve years old. Fees are generally $5 per hour per child and parents must remain on the premises. The Gold Coast offers three and a half hours of free child care for potty-trained two to eight year olds.

To be licensed, a child care facility generally must have a ratio of one supervising adult to each ten children. Personnel are subject to fingerprint checks, and no one with a criminal record can be on the staff. All caregivers must pass tuberculosis testing, learn CPR, and attend classes on recognizing and reporting child abuse/neglect. The facility is also subject to inspection by the Department of Health.

The ages of children accepted, rates per hour, and hours the facilities are open vary. At MGM Grand, where guests have priority and pay $2 less than nonguests, children from age three to twelve can stay for up to five hours or for two five-hour periods with a two-hour break between them. Rates for children whose parents are not hotel guests are from $8 to $9 per hour per child.

It's also possible to arrange through the hotel to have sitters stay with the children in your hotel room. **Vegas Valley Baby-sitters** (702/871-5161) offers twenty-four hour hotel in-room service. The four-hour minimum is $44 for one or two children plus $9 for each additional hour. If there are three children in the family, the cost is $44 for four hours and $10 for each additional hour. For four children in a family, it's $50 for four hours and $11 for each additional hour. Fees are higher for the holidays. These sitters, too, are checked for criminal records and are supposed to have passed TB tests and know CPR. To check on the accreditation of a day care facility or firm that supplies hotel-room sitters, parents can call the Clark County Child Care Licensing Department at 702/455-3894.

Health Care

It is reassuring to know in advance what help is available should a medical emergency arise while you're on vacation. Travelers of all ages can take comfort in the fact that Inn-House Doctor, Inc. offers free telephone consultations (702/259-1616). If necessary, the doctors make hotel visits.

One of the predominant health hazards to tourists is dehydration. Las Vegas is located at the point where three deserts—the Mojave, Sonoran, and Great Basin—meet. That means the atmosphere is very dry; so dry that you don't realize that you're perspiring because the perspiration evaporates so quickly. Therefore, be sure that everyone has his or her own water bottle and drinks from it frequently. Hats, sunscreen, and sunglasses offer protection from sunburn and eyestrain.

Another "ounce of prevention" strategy is to start briefing children in advance as to what to do in case they should become separated from the rest of the group. That way you'll be able to reinforce your message so that they won't panic in case the theoretical becomes reality. Also make sure to pin your children's names and addresses in their pockets if they aren't old enough to transmit that information. If you plan to rent a car, as soon as you take possession of it, have each child who is old enough memorize the license number in case you sometimes meet at the car. You can't imagine how many white GEO rentals there are in Las Vegas—in a large parking lot you can pass a half dozen of them on the way to the one you've rented.

Money Matters

Whether or not your wallets are packed with maximum-limit platinum cards, sometime in the course of your planning you'll have to decide how much money in traveler's checks and cash to bring along. Although credit cards are accepted at most hotels, motels, and restaurants in Las Vegas, you will need cash for vending machines, some amusements such as video arcades, tips, some food sources, and attractions, as well as events such as festivals.

It's difficult to cash personal checks unless there's a branch of your bank located in Las Vegas or your hotel has a policy of cashing checks for hotel guests. There are ATMs galore, however, at supermarkets, at drugstores, at banks, and in most casinos. So if you don't mind paying the fees and have one of the major ATM cards—Plus, Cirrus, Global Access, Starr, MasterCard, or Explore—you shouldn't have any trouble getting supplemental funds.

Major banks in Las Vegas are: Wells Fargo, 60 locations; Bank of America, about forty branches or ATM locations; California Federal (Cal Fed), with four locations; Citibank Nevada, six locations; and First Security Bank, 13 locations. Most banks are open

9:00 A.M. to 5:00 P.M., Monday–Thursday; 9:00 A.M. to 5:30 P.M., Friday; 10:00 A.M. to 1:00 P.M., Saturday.

Tipping Tips

When you're visiting Las Vegas as a family, life becomes much easier if you take advantage of various services that are offered. Many of the people who perform these services for you earn minimum wage and rely on tips to survive. The following guide will help you decide how much to tip when satisfactory service has been rendered:

- *Bell captains and bellmen:* Tip $1 or $2 dollars per bag; around $5 if you have several bags.
- *Hotel concierge:* If you have the concierge make several arrangements (for shows, car rental, and the like) a tip of $5 is appropriate.
- *Housekeeping help:* When maids bring extra pillows, an ironing board and iron, or fulfill other requests, a $1 or $2 tip will be appreciated for each special trip they make to your room. Amazingly, many hotel guests take these services for granted. It's also a kind gesture, whenever you leave your rooms in more than normal disarray, to compensate maids for the extra time it takes to get them looking neat again, with a dollar or two per day or a gratuity when you check out.
- *Pool attendants:* Tip $.50 to $1.00 when they perform a service, such as bringing you a towel.
- *Restaurant waitpersons:* Anything from 12 to 20 percent is the norm and should depend upon the quality of service received.
- *Room service:* 12 to 20 percent is usual.
- *Taxi drivers:* You should tip $1 (or $1 and change) when the fare is below $10; 10 to 15 percent when it's more than that.

- *Tour guides:* $1 to $2 per person at the end of the tour is the norm.
- *Valet parking:* $1 when the car is brought to you is usual, but $2 given to the attendant along with your claim ticket generally gets your car to you faster.
- *Warming the baby's bottle:* Though this is part of the regular service on an airplane, in a restaurant it's an extra. Add $.50 to $1.00 to your regular tip.

Although some visitors tip in anticipation of services, you should in most cases get good service without tipping before the fact. An exception is at entertainments in showrooms that have restaurant-style (as opposed to theater-style with seat numbers on the tickets) seating. In these situations, it's customary to tip the maitre d' $5 to $20 in advance, which might get you better seating than you would otherwise receive.

Clipping Coupons

Las Vegas is a coupon clipper's paradise. The free weekly and monthly entertainment magazines, the airline in-flight magazines, and the daily newspaper, as well as brochures and other printed material at the tourist information centers all contain coupons. Some of them are for free souvenirs or food; others are for discounts on food, attractions, or shopping. They may offer two admissions (or food items) for the price of one; a certain dollar amount; or percentage discount on specific attractions or merchandise; or a free item with the purchase of another item.

If you're interested in saving money and willing to devote a little time to the project (some kids love cutting out the coupons and tagging along while the adults collect the freebies or twofers), you'll be able to do very well. You'll find discounts for several of the major attractions in a variety of publications. Two-for-one show tickets and two-for-one city tours, as well as twofers to sights in the surrounding area, are also readily available. In fact, discounts are available on almost every tour of Las Vegas and its environs.

To get a head start on collecting your coupons, write for the "Discover Nevada Bonus Book," available from the Nevada Commission on Tourism (Capitol Complex, Carson City, NV 89710; 775/687-4322).

CHAPTER 2

Bedding Down

With more than 125,000 hotel and motel rooms to choose from, deciding which one best suits your family's Las Vegas vacation can be puzzling. Choices range from posh suites in high-rise hotel/casinos to no-frills rooms in mom-and-pop motels, with a number of other options that you might not have thought about.

Making the right accommodations choice is of greater importance to your vacation's success when three or more people are involved than it is for a couple of adults—especially when some of those people are small children. Spending an hour or two researching the various lodging possibilities and comparing them with your family's needs and expectations will go a long way to ensure that you choose those accommodations that work best for you.

Kids that spend their happiest hours swimming may not much care where they sleep so long as the pool has a great slide. But don't count on their being able to swim from mid-November to mid-February, since most hotel/motel pools are outdoors, which can make for some mighty chilly dips (many of the pools are closed during this period).

Preteens and teenagers' top priority may be proximity to

shopping. And if they're responsible enough to let loose on their own, you'll want accommodations located so that your young shoppers can safely walk to a mall or a shopping arcade.

If your youngsters need lots of running-around room, properties close to expanses of grass where playing is permitted will make life easier. Since light sleepers may be awakened by the coming and going of hotel/casino guests at all hours, their parents will rest easier, too, in quieter locations.

Some kids are endlessly fascinated watching the Strip from their thirty-second-floor hotel room windows; others equate entertainment with the television tube. You know your children better than anyone else does, so use your good judgment combined with perceptions of what you want your family to get out of the Las Vegas experience.

Hotel/Casino Accommodations

Because hotel accountants' statistics show that the average adult in each guest room spends a certain number of dollars in the casino downstairs, rates for hotel/casino rooms and suites are generally less expensive than those for hotels in other metropolitan areas. They also often cost less than Las Vegas motel rooms with comparable amenities. Rooms whose weekday rates start at $75 and under are considered inexpensive; $75 to $125, moderate; and $125 and up, expensive. Weekend rates are often much higher.

Although there are more than two dozen hotel/casinos on the Strip, and several more on the drawing boards or under construction, not all of them are the sorts of places children and teenagers will enjoy. The following, however, are real kidpleasers.

Circus Circus Hotel Casino (2880 Las Vegas Boulevard S.; 800/634-3450) was the first major Las Vegas property to cater to families and is considered the city's best value in budget accommodations. The midway is the main draw, with aerialists flying through the air, clowns riding motorcycles, and highwire walkers providing free entertainment hourly from 11:00 A.M. until midnight.

Traditional carnival midway games still convince the youngsters that it's easy to win the stuffed animal prizes—they're sure that it's a cinch to knock over the milk bottles or get the basketball through the hoop. Less expensive with loads of laughs are the funhouse mirrors you can pose in front of for free.

Circus Circus's five-acre indoor theme park, completed in 1993, is especially popular with elementary school–age children. The climate-controlled Grand Slam amusement park features 140-foot sandstone cliffs, tunnels, grottoes, and a waterfall. Canyon Blaster claims to be the only double-loop, double-corkscrew indoor roller coaster in the United States. The Rim Runner, a water flume ride, careens down a mountain and through a tunnel, splashing all the way. At Twist and Shout, kids ride rafts through twisting tubes, and at Hot Shots they play laser tag in a futuristic environment. Height requirement for the Canyon Blaster is forty-eight inches and there's a forty-two-inch requirement for the rest of the rides.

Other attractions include a net climb and ball crawl area, as well as a miniature roller coaster, the Fossil Dig play area, and an airplane ride for smaller children.

The rooms aren't fancy but are a good value for the money, starting at less than $60 and costing even less with late November/ December promotions. There are eight restaurants and snack bars on the premises, including the Steak House, which has an excellent reputation, and a McDonald's.

If I were a kid again, chances are I would beg to stay at **Excalibur Hotel & Casino** (3850 Las Vegas Boulevard S.; 800/937-7777 or 702/597-7777). With turrets and towers, flying pennants, a moat, and a drawbridge, it's every child's idea of a medieval castle, even though the hotel towers are twenty-eight-stories high. At the rear entrance, a glockenspiel fairy tale is played out over the giant clock each hour from 10:00 A.M. until

10:00 P.M. daily. Inside the hotel/casino, the medieval theme is carried out with banners, heraldic shields, strolling minstrels, fair maidens, jugglers, and jesters.

On the lower level, arcade games have a medieval twist. My favorite is the horse race, with players sitting at a long counter facing the racecourse. When the signal is given, each player rolls a ball into holes with various point values, with each successful toss moving a knight in armor and his steed forward. The player whose knight reaches the finish line first wins a small toy. If you keep paying your money and winning, you can win bigger toys (you could buy similar toys for a lot less money, but it wouldn't be nearly so exciting). The two-for-one arcade game coupons, which are frequently passed out in the hotel's shopping areas, can help stretch the kids' spending money.

At the Magic Motion Machine, also on the lower level, two 48-seat motion-simulator theaters provide exciting rides that last three minutes. On the upper level, there's free continuous entertainment for the whole family on the Court Jester's Stage daily from 10:00 A.M. to 10:00 P.M.

There's also the Medieval Village on the second floor, with shops and restaurants. At one stand you can have your pictures taken in medieval costumes; at another, your photo is transferred to the cover of a magazine or on a T-shirt. Free second-floor entertainment is provided by strolling Renaissance performers, including magicians, musicians, and puppeteers. It's also fun to stand outside the Canterbury Wedding Chapel and watch brides, grooms, and their wedding parties all dressed up in medieval garb.

With 4,032 rooms, Excalibur is one of the country's largest hotels, so it's not the place for people who are uncomfortable in crowds. Rates are in the inexpensive-to-moderate range, depending on the season. Ten restaurants and snack bars offer everything from coffee shop fare to a dinner show with a medieval theme.

Junior Egyptologists will enjoy **Luxor Las Vegas Hotel and**

Casino (3900 Las Vegas Boulevard S.; 800/288-1000 or 702/262-4000), the pyramid-shaped hotel/casino that lays claim to the "world's largest atrium." There's also a ten-story sphinx at the front entrance and a 3,000-foot interior waterway that hotel guests can travel along.

Luxor's interactive experiences get high marks from both children and adults. A full-scale replica of King Tut's Tomb and museum containing Egyptian artifacts are among its attractions (see chapter 6).

The Luxor contains 4,474 guest rooms, which include 484 suites. Rates are in the moderate range. Nine theme restaurants include Pharoah's Dinner Theater, Papyrus (Polynesian dishes), Oasis (poolside lunches), and the Sacred Sea Room (seafood). Room rates are usually in the moderate range, but like those at most Las Vegas hotels, they climb precipitously when the town is packed.

MGM Grand Hotel and Casino (3799 Las Vegas Boulevard S.; 800/929-1111 or 702/891-1111) opened in December 1993 and was revamped in 1997–1998 to the tune of $250 million. Its thirty-three-acre theme park has been significantly downsized, and now is used only for group events. With five thousand rooms, the hotel is the world's second largest. Among the more than a dozen eateries you'll find a McDonald's, a Taco Bell, and, at the high end, a Wolfgang Puck cafe. Room rates are high-moderate to expensive.

The **Venetian Resort and Casino** (3355 Las Vegas Boulevard S.; 702/414-1000), which opened in 1999, will appeal to teenagers more than to little tots, though the latter will like riding in the gondolas and watching the straw-hatted gondoliers on the 1,200-foot Grand Canal. The 3,036-suite Venetian features Venice's famous landmarks incorporated into its architecture, some fifty Canal Shoppes and restaurants including Stephan Pyle's Star Canyon, Emeril Lagasse's Delmonico Steakhouse, and Wolfgang Puck's Postrio.

Mandalay Bay (3950 Las Vegas Boulevard S.; 702/632-7777) also opened in 1999. Water babies, as well as their big brothers and sisters, will have a splashing good time at the resort's extensive swimming complex. You can't take advantage of the wave pool, lazy river, sand beach, huge swimming pool, and other neat features unless you're staying at Mandalay Bay or Four Seasons, however.

Paris Resort and Casino (3655 Las Vegas Boulevard S.; 702/946-7000). This new property doesn't have a lot of features other than the pool to appeal to youngsters, but they may think the replica of the Eiffel Tower and Mongolfier balloon are pretty cool.

Aladdin Resort and Casino (3667 Las Vegas Boulevard S.; 702/785-5555). Kids that continually beg to be dropped off at the mall will adore Desert Passage, which adjoins Aladdin. The bicycle-propelled pedicabs and lots of interesting shops such as Build a Bear Workshop, Cashman's Photo Magic, the Endangered Species Store and Houdini's Magic Shop (see page 70) will keep them occupied for hours. The thirty-nine-story, 2,567-room Aladdin is the most recent addition to the Strip.

Though the **Mirage** (3400 Las Vegas Boulevard S.; 800/627-6667 or 702/791-7111) is essentially a hotel/casino for adults, it incorporates several attractions that children like. Out front, the centerpiece of the five-acre lagoon is a volcano-waterfall that spews fire one hundred feet above the water several times each night (weather permitting). Surrounding the lagoon, the hotel/casino's front gardens provide an oasis of palm trees, orchids, and tropical plants.

Near the casino entrance, Siegfried & Roy's royal white tigers prowl in a habitat especially created for them. Behind the front desk, surgeonfish, puffers, triggerfish, and rays along with dozens of other species of tropical fish, swim in a 20,000-gallon tank. Even more popular is the dolphin habitat in the resort's garden. The admission charge includes a short guided tour of the special marine facility, which contains more than one million gallons of man-made seawater and seven Atlantic bottle-nosed dolphins.

The mammals can be viewed both above and below water level from 9:00 A.M. to 7:00 P.M. on weekends and from 11:00 A.M. to 7:00 P.M. on weekdays.

The Mirage showroom (Siegfried & Roy Theatre) is the venue for the famous and super-expensive "Siegfried & Roy" show (see chapter 9).

Accommodations at the Mirage include 3,049 guest rooms, 260 suites, eight villa apartments, and six bungalows. The latter have their own kitchens and private pools. Rates are in the expensive range. Nine places serve food within the hotel/casino and its grounds; Japanese, Chinese (Cantonese and Szechuan), northern Italian, and West Indian food are among the specialties.

Only in Las Vegas could the Empire State Building rub shoulders with the Statue of Liberty, but at **New York-New York** (3790 Las Vegas Boulevard S.; 702/740-6969) ten Manhattan landmarks cuddle up together to form the hotel/casino on eighteen acres. They're smaller than life (the Empire State Building is 529 feet tall, half of its actual height), but impressive nonetheless—especially with people who've never been to the Big Apple.

Inside, re-creations of Greenwich Village, Broadway, SoHo, and Little Italy's streets meander through slot machines and blackjack table areas, complete with brownstones, fire escapes, street lamps, ornamental ironwork, and graffiti. The mezzanine is a Las Vegas take on Coney Island with the latest in video games and Nathan's hot dogs. But the most popular mezzanine spot is the subway-turnstile entrance to the Manhattan Express roller coaster. It's rated by roller coaster experts as one of the greatest anywhere (it hits top speeds of 67 mph), but has had some mechanical problems in the past. Views from the top—for people brave enough to keep their eyes open—include Excalibur's turrets, the MGM lion, and Tropicana's islands.

With 2,035 rooms, six restaurants, and a food court, New York-New York is one of the smaller of the newer properties on the Strip. Room rates are in the expensive range.

Despite all the new arrivals on the theme hotel scene,

Treasure Island (3300 Las Vegas Boulevard S.; 800/944-7444 or 702/894-7111), remains my favorite. Mainly, I suppose, because it's so imaginative. Instead of a regular sidewalk out front, there's a gangway with rope-rigged railings. Lying at anchor in the moat are a pirate ship and the British frigate *Royal Brittania,* which do battle every afternoon and evening unless the weather doesn't cooperate (the pirate ship always wins). And the front facade of the casino, reminiscent of Disneyland's "Pirates of the Caribbean," looks like some island community in the West Indies where the pirates might put in to port. In short, the place is a natural for kids who are enthralled with the likes of Long John Silver and Captain Hook.

The casino—which you have to walk through to get to the guest room elevators—features a swashbuckling decor with ships' mastheads, buccaneer's booty, and other items that pirate wannabes think are cool.

The swimming pool has an exciting two-hundred-foot slide, and there's also Mutiny Bay—an 18,000-square-foot entertainment center with video games, pinball machines, and electronically simulated rides. Kids who are frequent visitors may find it advantageous to join the Mutiny Bay Club. Patterned after the slot clubs for adults, members are given cards that they can insert in the machines each time they play. Points earned accumulate and can be redeemed for prizes.

Rates for the tastefully furnished rooms ordinarily are in the high-moderate range; those on the upper floors have spectacular views of the Strip at night. Restaurants' names sustain the pirate theme—Black Spot Grille, Buccaneer Bay Club (continental cuisine), The Plank (steaks and seafood), Seven Seas Snack Bar, Smugglers Cantina (Mexican food), and Sweet Revenge (ice cream).

Though **Tropicana Resort & Casino** (3801 Las Vegas Boulevard S.; 800/634-4000 or 702/739-2222) was definitely designed with adults in mind, kids love it, too. Especially those who practically live in the water. There are three swimming pools—

one of which is billed as the "largest indoor-outdoor pool in the world." You'll find fish ponds, thirty waterfalls, and lagoons populated by flamingos, penguins, and swans in the five-acre tropical pool area. Carvings of two Maori gods that weigh three hundred thousand pounds each and stand 350 feet tall dominate the outer island, with jungle sounds and island music adding to the tropical ambience.

The 425-foot walkway between the two hotel towers is lined with cages containing live macaws, toucans, and parrots. Twelve-minute music and laser light shows, presented six times nightly March through October, are another attraction that's popular with youngsters.

Room rates at the Tropicana are in the moderate range, and on-premise eateries include a pizzeria, a deli, and a Baskin-Robbins ice cream counter. There's a game arcade, too.

An additional advantage of staying at Excalibur, Luxor, Tropicana, MGM Grand, and New York-New York is that they are within easy walking distance of one another. They're also served by monorail (from MGM Grand to Bally's two very long blocks up the Strip) and tram (between Luxor and Excalibur). Pedestrian overpasses remove the hazards of playing pedestrian roulette with the traffic at Las Vegas Boulevard and Tropicana, the city's busiest intersection.

You may have a hard time enticing your swimmers away from the 21,000-square-foot pool area at **Monte Carlo** (3770 Las Vegas Boulevard S.; 800/311-8999 or 702/730-7777), which includes waterfalls, a pool and spa, a children's pool, a wave pool, and "Lazy River." The river has an island in the center, and slight current action gently pulls swimmers along. Telling the kids that lunch will be at the Monte Carlo's food court—concessions include Haagen Daz, McDonald's, Nathans, Sbarro's (pizza), and Golden Bagels—may help to persuade them to get out of the pool.

The Monte Carlo is one of the most tastefully decorated of the hotel/casinos, and it is a joint venture of Mirage Resorts and

Circus Circus Enterprises, two of the most highly respected companies in the gaming industry. The hotel contains 3,014 rooms and 255 suites, with guest room prices in the inexpensive to expensive range, depending on days of week and dates (a typical situation in Las Vegas).

Caesars Palace (3570 Las Vegas Boulevard S.; 800/634-6001 or 702/731-7110), with its Forum Shops, is the perfect accommodations choice for a family of shopaholic teenagers with lots of bucks. Car-crazy kids who stay at the **Imperial Palace** (3535 Las Vegas Boulevard S.; 800/634-6441 or 702/794-3174) will spend hours gazing at the two hundred antique, classic, and special interest automobiles on the fifth floor of the hotel's parking facility.

Bellagio (3600 Las Vegas Boulevard S.; 702/693-7111) is a beautiful hotel, but not especially family-friendly. In fact, the hotel has a policy that nonguests under the age of eighteen may only be in the hotel when accompanied by parents with reservations at one of the property's restaurants, the art gallery, or for the showroom production "*O*."

Some of the other adult-oriented properties aren't so overt in discouraging family groups, but nonetheless they aren't the sorts of places that will appeal to children. It's therefore a good idea when you inquire about rates to ask if the hotel has any attractions especially designed for youngsters.

Off-Strip and Neighborhood Hotel/Casinos

As space on the Strip gets scarce—and ultraexpensive—hotel/casino developers have become more enthusiastic about off-Strip locations that are an easy hike to Las Vegas Boulevard and the city's major action.

One of the more recent arrivals on the off-Strip scene, the **Hard Rock Hotel and Casino** is a big hit with teenagers. And no wonder. Even though they can't loiter in the casino area, kids can walk around the interior periphery, which is crammed with rock-and-roll memorabilia. At the entrance is a giant chandelier, with saxophones as its pendants. In cases lining the walls you will find performance jackets worn by Motley Crue, Meatloaf, Iggy Pop, and Tommy Lee Jones. Another case features White Zombie's onstage get-ups, including a rather obscene vest with all sorts of rude sayings and images decorating it. The drum set played by Eric Kretz with Stone Temple Pilots and a custom Hardtail Springer owned by Nikki Sixx of Motley Crue (it originally was a Hell's Angels bike) are among the larger items on display.

In a city that contains nine of the world's ten largest hotels, the Hard Rock Hotel and Casino is a very small one with only 340 rooms, but expansion is on the way. It also has a rare Las Vegas feature that fresh-air fans will welcome—windows that you can actually open. Rooms, which are in the expensive range, are especially hard to get during the March–April spring break periods. It's the world's first and only rock 'n roll hotel and casino.

Though the **Rio Suite Hotel & Casino** (3700 Flamingo Road; 800/PLAYRIO or 702/252-7777) doesn't have a lot of features especially designed with children in mind, this South American–themed property is a big hit with youngsters when it comes to mealtimes. The restaurant atop the forty-one-story tower offers eagle-eye views of Las Vegas; the Carnival World Buffet features dishes from eleven countries.

Parents who like to spend some time at the slots and gaming tables and have small children may find it handy to stay at the **Orleans Hotel & Casino** (4500 W. Tropicana Avenue; 800/331-5334 or 702/365-7111; pronounced *Orleens*), where bonded child care personnel look after youngsters in the hotel's child care facility. The service is free to guests for a period of up to two hours each day of their stay.

A handful of "neighborhood" hotel/casinos and several more along the Boulder Highway offer still more accommodation options. Of the neighborhood hotel/casinos, **Texas Station** (2101 Texas Star Lane; 800/654-8888 or 702/631-1000) is one that is likely to appeal to youngsters. The decor is honkytonk Southwest, re-creating the storefronts of a western movie set. Restaurants are informal, and the Texas 12 Theater shows movies on fourteen screens.

Another neighborhood hotel/casino, the **Santa Fe** (4949 N. Rancho Drive; 800/872-6823 or 702/658-4900) is sure to be a winner with youngsters who love to ice skate since the property contains a year-round ice skating rink (see chapter 7). Also featured are a bowling center, a video arcade, and a nursery center on the premises for children six months to six years.

A clutch of hotel/casinos along Boulder Highway on the eastern edge of the city provide more accommodation options. **Sam's Town Hotel & Gambling Hall** (5111 Boulder Highway; 800/634-6371 or 702/456-7777) features a fifty-six-lane bowling center; the largest western wear retail store west of the Mississippi, and a 25,000-square-foot indoor park with waterfalls, a "mountain," and lots of footpaths to follow, plus a sand volleyball layout and big swimming pool. There's also a supervised playroom for children from two to eight years of age.

Another Boulder Highway property that welcomes children is **Boulder Station** (4111 Boulder Highway; 800/683-7777 or 702/432-7777). Among its features are a video arcade, a state-of-the-art eleven-plex theater complex called ACT III, and Kids Quest child care (see chapter 1, Time Out). Boulder Station's sibling, **Sunset Station** (1301 W. Sunset Road; 702/547-7777) is one of the newest hotel/casinos in town—an advantage as far as the freshness of the rooms is concerned, especially those where smoking is allowed. Sunset Station is right across the street from Galleria at Sunset shopping mall.

Hyatt Regency Lake Las Vegas (101 Montelago Boulevard, Henderson; 702/567-1234). With Mediterranean–North African décor and set on a lovely man-made lake seventeen miles from the Strip, this hotel is lovely and a favorite with golfers. It also has Camp Hyatt, a children's program that features supervised play and activities for youngsters aged three to twelve. The program offers second rooms at half-price (based on availability) and a specially priced children's menu as well as day-time and evening camp activities.

Downtown Lowdown

I can think of only two reasons for a family with no gambling members to stay at a downtown Glitter Gulch hotel/casino. One of those reasons is that the **Golden Nugget Hotel & Casino** (129 Fremont Street; 800/634-3454 or 702/385-7111) offers the best accommodations value in town—it's a four-star hotel with double room rates as low as $59 a night. The food served at the Golden Nugget's coffee shop and restaurants is also better than you'll get at most casino eateries.

The second reason is the pedestrians-only portion of Fremont Street and its nightly sound and light extravaganza, Fremont Street experience (see chapter 6). Though the show lasts for only eight minutes of each hour during the evening, the malled street makes for pleasant strolling before and after. And the thousands of yards of colored neon tubing and the flashing and pulsating lights of the casinos should enthrall everybody. After all, where else in the world is it so bright that can you read a newspaper outdoors at midnight or find so much over-the-top glitz and glitter to gawk at?

Non-Gaming Accommodations

Some family groups may prefer to stay at a hotel or motel away from the gambling palaces. If you want to de-emphasize gaming, the last thing you need is to have to walk through part of the casino every time you want to go to or from your hotel room. One of the best value-for-money motels is **Fairfield Inn by Marriott** (3850 S. Paradise Road; 702/791-0899). **La Quinta Inn Convention Center** (3970 S. Paradise Road; 702/796-9000), **Residence Inn by Marriott** (3225 S. Paradise Road; 702/796-3000), **Courtyard by Marriott** (3275 Paradise Road; 800/321-

2211 or 702/791-3600), and the all-suite **Holiday Inn-Crowne Plaza** (4255 Paradise Road; 800/654-2000 or 702/369-4400) are among the better non-casino accommodations that are more expensive. **Polo Towers** (3745 Las Vegas Boulevard S.; 702/261-1000) contains condo units, which are rented nightly when not occupied by time-share owners.

The Four Seasons Hotel (3960 Las Vegas Boulevard S.; 702/632-5000), which opened in 1999, is the only hotel without a casino on the Strip. Room rates in the five-star, 400-room property are in the expensive range. However, it's the most child-friendly hotel in town. Upon arrival, each child is presented with a welcome basket, which contains goodies such as stuffed animals, T-shirts, and baseball caps. Kids are also given milk and cookies or popcorn and soda at check-in. Board and video games are available for their use and automatic child proofing of rooms is done prior to their arrival. The program is complimentary.

Bargain-Hunting Advice

Rates at all Las Vegas hotels and motels vary with demand and can change from one hour to the next. Rooms that cost $50 on a slow weekday in December can cost four times that much on a busy weekend in April. As a rule, you'll get more value for money on winter weekdays; the least, during prime weather and when big conventions or trade shows are in town.

Securing your reservations well in advance allows you to lock in rates that might not be available later. If you find close to the departure date that you can get a better deal elsewhere, take it and cancel the first reservation.

Half-price clubs such as **Traveler's Advantage** (40 Oakview Street, Trumbull, CT 06611; 800/445-4137) work best, also, when you can make your plans far in advance. The half-price hotel booklet that comes with a Traveler's Advantage membership (approximately $50 a year) lists two dozen hotels and motels in Las Vegas, but you can be sure rooms won't be available at many of them except during the winter or on occasional weekdays at other times of the year, unless you're able to reserve well in advance.

You might also want to investigate packages put together by airlines in conjunction with various Las Vegas hotels. America West Vacations, for example, combines air transport to Las Vegas from a number of U.S. cities with accommodations at any of thirteen hotels, including New York-New York, MGM Grand, and Excalibur. Prices vary according to dates.

Alternative Accommodations

If you'd rather sleep under the stars than the bright lights, consider renting a houseboat on nearby Lake Mead and commuting into the city when you feel like taking in the man-made attractions.

The houseboats—some models sleep as many as fourteen people—come air conditioned and fully furnished. All you need to bring on board are groceries and ice. And anglers who have any luck at all will be able to augment the store-bought groceries with bluegill, crappie, striped or large mouth bass, catfish, and trout.

Houseboats are furnished with breakfast bars, dining tables, or both. Sleeping quarters feature everything from bunks to queen-size beds. There are sun decks (with and without awnings), stereos, TVs, VCRs, microwaves, and gas barbecue grills.

Two companies—**Seven Crown Resorts** (800/752-9669 or 714/588-7100) and **Forever Resorts** (800/255-5561 or 702/565-4813) rent houseboats. Seven Crown operates out of the Echo Bay Marina on the northern arm of the lake and Forever Resorts from Callville Bay on the western shore of the same arm. The drive into Las Vegas from the marinas takes from forty-five minutes to an hour.

Generally, rental periods are three, four, or seven days. Seven Crown Resorts rates are lowest during the coolest months (from $850 for four-day rentals of houseboats that sleep six to $1,950 for those that sleep fourteen). Peak season, when four-day rentals of the same houseboats are $1,250 and $2,450, is June 15 through September 15. Since temperatures can hit 110 degrees Fahrenheit and higher during these months, it's the least pleasant time of the year as far as many Las Vegas visitors are concerned.

Forever Resorts divides the year into four seasons—value (January 1 to April 31, October 2 to December 31); spring (May 1 to June 4); regular (June 1 to September 1, Memorial and Labor Day weekends); and fall (September 1 to October 19). Four-day rates for a houseboat that sleeps ten range from $995 to $1,295 (weekday/weekend rental) in value season to $2,095 to $2,295 in regular season (with $1,595 to $1,795 in the spring and $1,795 to $2,195 in the fall).

RVers have a choice of several parks, ranging in price from $12 to $30 a night. Two of the better parks adjacent to casinos are: **Circusland RV Park** (500 Circus Circus Drive; 800/634-3450 or 702/794-3757) and **Sam's Town RV Park** (5111 Boulder Highway; 800/634-6371 or 702/454-8055).

Among the nicer non-casino RV parks is **KOA Campgrounds-Las Vegas Resort** (4315 Boulder Highway; 702/451-5527), with complimentary shuttle service to the Strip, a playground, a store, and a pool. There are also several campgrounds at Lake Mead. Members-only RV parks that have campgrounds in the Las Vegas area include **Thousand Trails** (429 S. Boulder Highway; 702/451-7632).

Campers can find places to pitch their tents in the Las Vegas orbit, too. There's a fifteen-tent site at Red Rock Canyon. Though it's difficult to find a space, if you do, you can stay for up to fourteen days. The best time to try for a spot is midday.

There are also tent sites at Mount Charleston and at various campgrounds around Lake Mead. Some of the campgrounds are free, others may have a small nightly fee. If you're interested in camping farther from Las Vegas, you might consider **Valley of Fire State Park.**

Least expensive *indoor* accommodations are usually at hostels, and there are three of them in Las Vegas. Most of the accommodations are dormitory style, but a few family rooms and semi-private rooms are available (see chapter 11 to obtain addresses and telephone numbers).

CHAPTER 3

Feeding Time

Whether you're looking for a fancy restaurant, coffee shop, fast-food, take-away, snack bar, deli, ice cream parlor, or buffet, you won't have to go far to find what you want. At last count, there were more than three thousand eateries in Clark County—most of them in Las Vegas.

The big hotel/casinos each have several restaurants on their premises—from inexpensive coffee shops and buffets to gourmet rooms. As a general rule, casino food is less expensive than are comparable meals served in non-casino restaurants; however, casino dining in general is not memorable. So if mealtimes play a major part in your family's vacation enjoyment, you'll probably get meals you enjoy more at restaurants that aren't affiliated with the gambling houses.

Grazing and Appraising the Buffets

Since the 1940s, buffets have been synonymous with Las Vegas casinos. Almost every hotel/casino has one, as the following list indicates. Tax has been built in to some of the prices; others don't include it. Hours of service vary. Generally, however, breakfast is served from 7:00 A.M. to 10:00 or 11:00 A.M; lunch from

11:00 A.M. until 2:00 or 3:00 P.M., and dinner from 4:00 P.M. to
9:00 or 10:00 P.M.

Buffet	Breakfast ($)	Lunch ($)	Dinner ($)	Brunch ($)
°Children's prices available.				
Aladdin Hotel & Casino	10.99	12.99	18.99	
Arizona Charlie's	3.75	4.75	6.75	
Weekend brunch				5.95
Bally's	9.95	11.99	15.99	
Sterling brunch				52.95
Bellagio	10.95	13.95	22.95	
Saturday, Sunday				18.50
°Boulder Station	4.99	6.99	9.99/10.99/15.99	
Sunday champagne brunch				8.99
Caesars Palace	9.99	11.99	16.99	
°Castaways		6.49	8.95/10.95/14.95	
°Circus Circus	5.49	6.49	7.99	
°Excalibur	7.49	8.49	8.49/9.99	
°Fiesta	4.99	6.49	9.99/13.99	
Fitzgerald's	5.99	5.99	9.99	
Flamingo Hilton		9.95	18.99	
Daily brunch				8.75
Fremont	4.99	6.49	9.99	
Tuesday, Friday, Saturday seafood buffet				14.99
Sunday champagne brunch				8.99
Gold Coast	3.95	5.95	8.45	
Golden Nugget	5.75	7.50	10.25	
Sunday champagne brunch				10.95
Harrah's	8.99	9.99	14.99	
Saturday, Sunday champagne brunch				14.99
Holiday Inn/Boardwalk	5.99	6.99	8.49	

Buffet	Breakfast ($)	Lunch ($)	Dinner ($)	Brunch ($)
°Children's prices available.				
°Imperial Palace	6.25/7.45	7.50	8.50/9.45	
Saturday-Sunday champagne brunch				8.45
Lady Luck	4.95	5.95	7.95	
° Las Vegas Hilton	8.99	9.99	13.99	
Saturday/Sunday champagne brunch				12.99
°Luxor	8.49	8.99	12.99	
°Main Street Station	4.99	6.99	9.99/10.99/13.99	
Saturday, Sunday brunch				7.99
Mandalay Bay	10.50	10.50	17.95	
Sunday champagne brunch				17.95
Mandalay Bay House of Blues Sunday gospel brunch				37.00
°MGM Grand	9.99	10.99	15.99	
°Mirage	8.95	9.95	14.95	
Sunday champagne brunch				14.95
°Monte Carlo	8.49	8.25	11.49	
Sunday champagne brunch				12.99
Nevada Palace	4.99	6.99	9.99	
Sunday brunch				6.99
The Orleans	5.45	6.95	9.95/13.95	
Sunday brunch				9.95
Palace Station	4.99	6.99	8.99/9.99	
Saturday/Sunday champagne brunch				8.99
Paris Las Vegas	10.95	14.95	21.95	
Sunday champagne brunch				21.95
Regent Las Vegas		6.99	9.99/13.99	
Saturday, Sunday brunch				9.99
Rio Suites Hotel & Casino	8.00	11.00	14.00/26.95	

Buffet	Breakfast ($)	Lunch ($)	Dinner ($)	Brunch ($)
°Children's prices available.				
Riviera	7.50	8.50	10.50	
Weekend champagne brunch				8.50
Sahara Hotel			6.49	5.49
Saturday, Sunday brunch				8.49
Sam's Town (Mon.–Fri.)	4.99	6.99	10.99	
Sunday champagne brunch				8.99
San Remo	7.95	7.95	9.95	
Sunday champagne brunch				7.95
Santa Fe Hotel & Casino	3.95	4.95	8.95/10.95/14.95	
Sunday brunch				14.99
Silverton	3.99	6.49	7.99/10.99	
Saturday, Sunday brunch				5.99/9.99
Stardust (Mon.–Fri.)	6.95	7.95	10.95	
Sunday champagne brunch				6.95
Stratosphere	5.99	6.99	9.99	
Suncoast	4.95	6.95	9.95	
Sunday brunch				9.95
°Sunset Station	4.99	6.99	9.99/10.99	
Saturday/Sunday champagne brunch				9.99
Terribles	4.99	6.99	9.99/12.99	
Sunday champagne brunch				8.99
°Texas Station	4.99	6.99	9.99/10.99	
Saturday/Sunday brunch				9.99
Treasure Island	6.99	7.50	11.50	
Saturday, Sunday champagne brunch				11.50
Tropicana			11.95/14.95	
Brunch				7.95
Saturday/Sunday champagne brunch				10.95
Westward Ho Casino	6.95	6.95	8.95	

Since they were introduced, buffets have been the casinos' loss leaders—get 'em in, feed 'em, and make your profit when they play the slots on the way out. The quality of the buffet items generally has gone down in recent years, however, especially those at the low end of the price range. So your best bet is to choose among the more expensive buffets, (they're still inexpensive when compared with buffets in other parts of the country). Those recommended by both locals and tourists include Caesars Palace Platinum Buffet, the Buffet at the Golden Nugget, and the Mirage Buffet at the Mirage.

Two less expensive buffets that are several cuts above the rest are Harrah's Galley Buffet and Carnival World Buffet at Rio Suite Hotel/Casino. At the latter, chefs at five different food stations dish up American, Brazilian, Chinese, East Indian, and Mexican specialties. There's a dessert station and live entertainment as well.

The more expensive Village Seafood Buffet in Masquerade Village at the Rio ($26.95) has the reputation of being tied with the Regent Las Vegas ($25.00) for the best-value seafood buffet in town. At the Rio, chefs at the American, Mexican, Italian, Chinese, and Mongolian serving stations each prepare their specialties including seafood fajitas, Mongolian barbecue of scallops, and shrimp. The Regent's strength lies in the quality and quantity of its seafood.

Even though the prices of Las Vegas buffets have risen significantly since the first edition of this book in 1998, two non-casino newcomers that offer great value for your money have come on the scene. Though part of a chain, at Sweet Tomatoes (2080 N. Rainbow Road; 702/648-1957 and 375 N. Stephanie Street; 702/933-1212) everything is prepared from scratch. More than a dozen tossed salads, including cobb salad and wonton chicken salad, and about four dozen salads that don't contain greens (Mongolian marinated vegetable salad and southern dill potato salad are two of them) give you as many or more options than you will find on the Strip. There are also more than two dozen different muffins and breads plus an equal number of soups and chili as well as a selection of hot pasta dishes. Desserts include fresh fruit, soft ice cream, frozen yogurt, cookies, and jello. The cost is $6.69 for lunch and $7.99 for dinner (children six to twelve pay $4.49, and those under six years of age eat free). Plus, you'll find discount coupons for adults in newspapers and free entertainment magazines.

Even less expensive, **Soup or Salad** (2051 North Rainbow Road; 702/631-2604 and 4022 S. Maryland Parkway; 702/792-8555) offers fewer choices, but still it's a deal because the food is good and the price is only $4.99. On Sundays, children six to twelve years of age eat for $.99 and those under six are free.

For more exotic fare, **Ghandi** (4080 Paradise Road; 702/734-0094) offers an eighteen-course East Indian all-you-can-eat lunch buffet including a soup and salad bar. Served Monday through Friday from 11:00 A.M. to 2:30 P.M., it costs $7.45.

The Theme Restaurants

Theme cafes were the fastest growing segment of the restaurant industry and experienced a Las Vegas explosion during the 1990s. Overpriced food, memorabilia of the rich and famous, and adjacent logo shops were de rigueur. Crowds were apparently overwhelmed by the noise and underwhelmed by the food, because of the six major theme restaurants that opened in Las Vegas during the period, only three have survived.

Oversized menus are featured at **Harley-Davidson** (3725 Las Vegas Boulevard S.; 702/740-4555); but then, who would expect anything but a huge menu at a restaurant whose facade is dominated by a twenty-foot-high Harley varooming out of its facade?

This restaurant, so far, represents the ultimate in themeing. As you might expect, the decor includes lots of cycles. Some of them are owned by celebrities such as Ann-Margret and Billy Joel; others are specialty models, such as the Lion Bike and the

Taxi Bike. There's the Captain America Bike from *Easy Rider* (restaurant patrons can have their photo taken sitting on it); framed photos of celebrities on their Harleys—Roy Rogers, Tanya Tucker, and Willie Nelson among them.

A collection of Harley gas tanks, each signed by a celeb (Mario Cuomo, Branford Marsalas, Deion Sanders, and Naomi Judd, for example) and full-size cycles suspended from a conveyor belt overhead also reinforce the theme. The ooh-and-aaher, however, is the American flag made of 44,000 links of chain that completely covers one wall.

That super-size menu is also themed to the max. Nonalcoholic drinks are called Designated Drivers, and beverages such as coffee, tea, and juice are called Standard Lubricants. Appetizers are called Kick Starts; side dishes are known as Side Cars. Big Bowl Roadside Greens are—you guessed it—salads. And so on. House specialties include the Harley Hog Sandwich, which pairs Carolina pulled pork with a brioche. There's also Harley Texas Style Beef Chili and Harley Roast Chicken. On the menu's back are a list of Harley-Davidson engine names and their eras, one of Harley-Davidson model types, and one that's called "Terminology of the Road." The latter explains what terms such as "hardtail," "chopper," and "springer" mean.

Planet Hollywood (the Forum Shops; 702/791-7827) is also themed to the rafters. With zebra-striped carpet, fake palm trees, and bright banquettes and tablecloths, the super-size restaurant is colorful and noisy. Tinseltown memorabilia hangs from the ceilings and decorates the walls—movie set props and costumes worn in box-office hits; framed posters of all-time greats, and photos of the stars.

Although there are lots of drinks—alcoholic and nonalcoholic—on the oversize menu, the choice of food items isn't as large as in most of the other theme restaurants. Among the more unusual dishes are Hollywood Salad (grilled chicken slices, bacon, chopped egg, blue cheese, beets, red onions, sliced olives, and croutons on greens with balsamic vinaigrette; chicken, spinach, and artichoke pizza; and L.A. Lasagna (fried pasta tubes filled with ricotta cheese, covered with parmesan garlic cream and tomato basil sauces). Planet Hollywood's back bar is designed to look like the laboratory of a mad scientist, and the Lava Bar is themed around monster movies; the drinks served at the two are named in keeping with their themes.

A **Hard Rock Cafe** is a Hard Rock Cafe, unless you're in Las Vegas. Though the restaurant opens at 11:00 A.M., customers are standing in line by 10:15. True, the food such as the Tupelo-style chicken and huge triple decker B.L.T. is reasonably priced, probably due to the restaurant's off-strip location at 4775 S. Paradise Road (702/733-7625). But food alone isn't what brings the multitudes in. In the city of excesses, this Hard Rock is bigger and more flamboyant than others.

Outside the Hard Rock, a gigantic eighty-foot-long, six-string guitar dominates the restaurant's exterior. Inside, photos, more guitars, platinum records, and other rock memorabilia cover the walls from the top of the wainscoted booths to the high ceilings where fans spin nonstop. The level of excitement is much greater than at the restaurant's counterparts in Copenhagen or Puerto Vallarta. Surrounded by Las Vegas glitz, it's hard to believe that the first link in this chain—granddaddy of all theme cafes—started out with Eric Clapton's guitar hanging on the back wall of a culinary dive in London.

If you're not in the mood for lunch or dinner, you can splurge on Hard Rock desserts, perhaps the Heath Bar Rain Forest Nut Crunch Sundae (a combination of Heath Bar ice cream, hot fudge, whipped cream, crushed Heath Bars, toasted Brazil nuts, and a cherry) or Chocolate Chip Cookie Pie. Forgo the desire to buy anything at the Hard Rock Cafe logo shop, however, because the merchandise selection is far more extensive at the logo shop of the Hard Rock Hotel, just a large parking lot away.

Most every one of the theme restaurants has a gift shop, where T-shirts, caps, mugs, magnets, boxer shorts, sweats, and an incredible number of other logo-related items are for sale. Retail sales are big income generators at the theme restaurants, defying the notion that advertisers have to be paid in order to push a product.

Holy Cow! (2423 Las Vegas Boulevard S.; 702/732-2697) definitely has a theme, but it's far more down to earth than its star-struck neighbors farther south on the Strip. The most conveniently located for tourists of all the restaurants in the Big Dog Hospitality Group, it's a combination restaurant/micro-brewery/bovine gift shop, and clever as it can be (see chapters 5 and 6). The menu includes hearty food at modest prices—such dishes as bratwurst served on a bun with fries and coleslaw, fish and chips, and rotisserie herb chicken. Another good bet is Joe's Special—a combination of ground beef, spinach, sauteed mushrooms, onions, and scrambled eggs. It's listed as a breakfast item but served with home fries all day long.

The **Peppermill** (2985 Las Vegas Boulevard S.; 702/735-4177) is known for good food and generous portions. With its moderate prices, it is the place to go if your family likes lots of choices. There are four hundred items on the menu, and the salads are especially good. Desserts, like Mud Pie a la mode, are tempting, too.

If your children enjoy dress-up dining in a sophisticated environment that won't totally unbalance your budget, try **Wild Sage Cafe** (600 E. Warm Springs Road; 702/944-7243) where entrees range from eggplant with roasted vegetables to charbroiled tenderloin of beef. **Cafe Nicolle** (4760 W. Sahara Avenue; 702/870-7675) with its smart red, white, and black décor, is a bit less expensive and as an added plus has outdoor dining.

The **Cheesecake Factory** at the Forum Shops (702/792-6888) is a real kid-pleaser with an eighteen-page menu that is illustrated like a beautiful picture book. Among the two-hundred items are Beverley Hills pizza salad, TexMex eggrolls, and triple chocolate brownie truffle cheesecake.

A Touch of Class

Families who appreciate elegance won't want to miss high tea at the **Four Seasons** (3960 Las Vegas Boulevard S.; 702/632-5000). Along with tea (lemonade or other beverages for the children), scones, strawberry jam, and lemon curd; salmon, egg, and other finger sandwiches; and petits fours are served on china with fine silverware. The tuxedo-clad piano player at the grand piano plays Broadway show tunes, and service is perfection. The Verandah Dining Room is also a good choice for meals as the atmosphere is serene and the food far better than that of most hotel dining rooms.

Ethnic Eateries

Though not all children are adventurous eaters, those who are will find Las Vegas's variety of ethnic restaurants fascinating. Not only are there the usual Chinese, Mexican, German, French, and Italian restaurants, with dishes that have become an expected part of the restaurant scene, there are others where dishes more recently introduced to this country, such as the Chinese *dim sum* and Italian *panini*, are featured. Add to them the restaurants where Cuban, African, Near and Middle Eastern, Lebanese, and East Indian dishes are served, and you'll have an enormous smorgasbord of choices.

When you're in the mood for traditional Chinese dishes, go to the **Chinatown Plaza** (4205 Spring Mountain Road; 702/221-8448), where you'll find the largest concentration of the 110 Asian restaurants listed in the Las Vegas Yellow Pages. Restaurants in the center include Chinatown Express, Kim Tar Seafood Restaurant, 168 Shanghai Restaurant, Pho VietNam Restaurant, Plum Tree Inn (Mandarin and Szechwan cuisine), and Sam Woo BBQ Restaurant.

At **Mamounia Moroccan Restaurant** (4632 S. Maryland Parkway; 702/597-0092), intricately woven carpets decorate the walls, and diners sit on pillows at low, ornate tables. They're served by waiters wearing kaftans and slippers, and entertained by belly dancers. It's probably not a restaurant younger children will enjoy, but it's a great place to take teenagers who are eager to learn about other cultures. Menu items include kebabs of chicken, beef, and lamb; Cornish game hens; lamb shanks; couscous; *pastillas* (ground chicken, almonds, and scrambled eggs topped with phyllo dough); and an extremely sweet dessert called *chabakia*. Dinners are moderately expensive at about $20.

Far less expensive and not at all fancy, **Middle Eastern Bazaar** (4147 S. Maryland Parkway; 702/731-6030) is patronized almost exclusively by people of Middle Eastern descent. There are a few tables at the front of the store and some outside where you can sit after placing your order at the take-out counter. Among the specialties are *filafel* served in pita bread, *gyros* (spiced meat sandwiches), *tabbouleh* (salad of grain and vegetables), and homemade ice cream that contains rose water, saffron, and pistachio nuts.

Ghandi (4080 Paradise Road; 702/734-0094) features dishes from five different regions of India in a setting of East Indian elegance (ask to be seated on the balcony). It's the most expensive of the three East Indian restaurants in Las Vegas, but worth the extra money. Among the dishes are *tandoori* chicken, which is marinated and cooked in a clay oven; raita, a cucumber and yogurt salad that softens the bite of the curries; and the traditional flat breads such as *naan*, which are also baked in clay ovens. **Montesano's** (Sahara West Center, 3441 West Sahara Avenue, No. B2; 702/876-0348) is an Italian sit-down restaurant and delicatessen that offers terrific food at reasonable prices. Deli sandwiches include hot and cold heroes and a great corned beef and swiss with cole slaw and thousand-island dressing. The dining room with framed memorabilia on the walls and black and red high-backed chairs has a menu that features such dishes as veal marsala and lobster ravioli. Pizzas come with the standard toppings as well as the more unusual such as fresh plum and goat cheese or artichoke, black olive, and mozzarella. Italian ices make an ideal dessert.

Chevy's Mexican Restaurant (702/434-8323) is a good dining choice for families who are in the vicinity of the Galleria at Sunset. With neon cactus indoors and an outdoor terrace with umbrella tables, the ambience is sophisticated south-of-the-border. The menu's "Create Your Own Combos" allows diners to mix and match their enchiladas, tacos, tamales, and chiles relleno. Pork carnitas and various wraps, such as mesquite-grilled chicken, salsa, rice, and beans wrapped in a spinach tortilla, are also on the bill of fare. The children's menu/placemat, which is covered with puzzles and pictures (it comes with crayons), offers six meal choices that include entree, fresh corn, fresh fruit, corn strips, soda, fruit juice, or milk, and complimentary ice cream cone for $3.95. There's also a kiddie rice and beans plate for $.95.

A more upscale Mexican eatery, **La Barca Seafood Restaurant** (2517 E. Lake Mead Boulevard, North Las Vegas; 702/657-9700) is also a good choice with supersize shrimp cocktails, ceviche, chopped clam tostadas, and other Mexican dishes with a seafood focus. La Barca is especially fun when a mariachi band is playing.

Plum Tree Inn (Chinatown Plaza; 702/873-7077) and **Chang's Restaurant** (Bally's Hotel/Casino, 3645 Las Vegas Boulevard S.; 702/739-4653) are two places where you'll find *dim sum*. The different varieties of these Hong Kong–style filled dumplings are brought tableside on a cart, and it's great fun to choose which ones you think you'll like best.

Panini (4811 S. Rainbow Boulevard; 702/365-8300) is the place to go for the Italian-style sandwiches served on special breads such as foccacia. Among the choices are grilled chicken, roasted peppers, and baby greens on foccacia, and buffalo mozzarella, roasted eggplant, tomato, basil, and baby greens on grilled country breads. The dessert favorite at Panini is *tiramisu*.

Most major hotel/casinos in town have one or more restaurants where ethnic foods are served. Italian and Chinese fare predominates with Bally's, Harrah's, Excalibur, MGM Grand, Riviera, Sahara, Sam's Town, Sands, and Sheraton Desert Inn—as well as restaurants in the new casinos—dishing up plates of pasta and veal piccante.

The Chinese restaurants in casinos range from the posh Empress Court at Caesars Palace, with menu items such as birds' nest soup and abalone, to the Emperor's Room at Lady Luck where you can order a mountain of egg rolls, chow mein, and so forth for less than $10. At least a dozen casinos serve Mexican food, too.

When an ethnic festival's going on while you're in town, you'll be able to sample authentic cuisine of other cultures. At the Japanese celebrations you'll find stalls where teriyaki, tempura, and bean buns are sold; at the Greek festivals, *dolmades* and *baklava*. *Carne asada* and *menudo* are favorites at Mexican fiestas, and at the International Festival you'll be able to feast on everything from polynesian lomi-lomi salmon to Russian *pierogi*.

Delis, Diners, and Drive-Throughs

One of the easiest ways to feed a crowd when you're busy going places and doing things is by patronizing places whose business depends on speedy service. The following are a sampling of the best you'll find in Las Vegas.

Samuel's Restaurant, Delicatessen, Bakery (2744 Green Valley Parkway, Henderson; 702/454-0565) is a kosher delicatessen and bakery, and considered to be one of the best in Las Vegas. Among the four dozen or so sandwiches on the menu are a double-decker pastrami, roast beef, and turkey; a hot corned beef and tongue combo with cole slaw and Thousand Island dressing; and a tuna melt with Swiss cheese on rye (most sandwiches cost from $4.50 to $8.95). Dinner specialties include stuffed cabbage and roast brisket of beef with potato pancake and applesauce. Homemade New York–style cheesecake is the standout dessert.

Another kosher deli is **Casba** (855 E. Twain Avenue; 702/791-3344), specializing in Mideast cuisine, although there are a few European dishes such as schnitzel on the menu. With wood tables, striped upholstery on the chairs, and framed pictures on its white walls, the deli is much more attractive inside than its exterior would indicate. Menu offerings are traditional—matzo ball soup, gefilte fish, chopped liver salad, shishliks, and kabobs—and it's a good place to eat if you aren't put off by the service, which is abrupt to the point of being rude.

You'll find most U.S. fast food franchises represented in Las Vegas, from more than three dozen McDonald's (seven have indoor soft-play areas) and seventeen Taco Bells to members of smaller regional chains.

The California-based **In-N-Out Burger,** with five locations in Las Vegas, is perhaps the best hamburger ($1.44 with tax) value in town. **Fatburger,** with corporate offices and six locations in the city, sells hamburgers that cost about a dollar more, but taste just like homemade.

In an annual poll, **Popeye's Chicken & Biscuits** (2421 W. Bonanza Road; 702/646-2883 and 4506 E. Bonanza Road; 702/531-8441) and **Hill Top House Supper Club** (3500 N. Rancho Drive; 702/645-9904) are Las Vegas residents' top picks for fried chicken. **Wienerschnitzel** (various locations including 4001 W. Sahara Avenue; 702/362-0418) gets the nod for the best hot dogs. Positively delicious submarine sandwiches are produced at **Capriotti's** (several locations including Frisco Plaza, 322 W. Sahara Avenue; 702/444-0229). Pastrami, corned beef, provolone, salami, roast beef, and all the other favorite ingredients are stacked on oh-so-fresh rolls. The small size must weigh about two pounds and is big enough for at least two people.

The perfect last course for any take-away meal is a box of assorted Krispy Kreme doughnuts. There are Krispy Kreme counters inside New York-New York and Excalibur and outside Treasure Island as well as at other casinos. The doughnuts come in about a dozen and a half delicious flavors (try the sour cream glazed).

Einstein Bros. Bagels (4624 S. Maryland Parkway; 702/795-7800, 9031 West Sahara Avenue; 702/254-0919, and other locations) is both child-friendly and economical. A small classic Caesar salad with homemade bagel croutons costs $1.79 and along with a cup of soup is $2.99. Bagels with a choice of flavored cream cheeses cost $1.59 each; with a butter blend called Shmear, $.79. Hummus sandwiches are $1.79; pizza melts (three cheeses plus pepperoni or tomato slices) are $2.99. The coffee shop–style restaurants are very pleasant, but if you want to do it yourself and eat your bagels alfresco, you can buy a baker's dozen bagels for $4.99 and a tub of cream cheese for $1.90.

For breakfast and more, you might try that long time kid-pleaser, **International House of Pancakes,** which has nine locations in Las Vegas. Or have traditional oven-baked pancakes at **Keuken Dutch** (6180 W. Tropicana Avenue; 702/368-1077), a restaurant with Dutch decor that specializes in dishes from the Netherlands. Prices are moderate at both restaurants. **Liberty Cafe** in White Cross Drugs (1700 Las Vegas Boulevard N.; 702/383-0101) is a Las Vegas old-timer where you can buy sandwiches and such at reasonable prices.

Something-for-Everyone Dining

Almost every one of Las Vegas's big shopping malls and several hotel/casinos include food courts, and eating in them is a very efficient way to catch a quick bite while you're shopping or seeing the sights on the Strip. But if you want more for your dining experience, without sacrificing the food court option, head for the **Green Valley Town Center** (4500 E. Sunset Road).

Kids love to eat at the outdoor tables surrounding a plip-plop fountain in the Center Courtyard, but each of the restaurants surrounding the courtyard has inside seating as well. Surrounding the courtyard are an eclectic mix of eateries—ideal for families who can't agree on the kind of food they want to eat. Following are a few.

The Crocodile Cafe (702/456-7880) features California cooking with international influences. Appetizers include house-made Mexican tortilla soup and Italian bruschetta. There are several salads, sandwiches, and pastas on the menu (try the grilled ahi sandwich or the herb-crusted salmon and tiger shrimp salad). Heartier fare includes grilled Cuban chicken breast with cinnamon, sliced almonds, raisins, fresh oregano, and chopped tomatoes, served with caramelized bananas, rice, and black beans.

The Jr. Croc's Kids Menu includes kids rigatoni, grilled chicken strips with crocodile fries, and cheese pizza. The menu/placemat comes with a pack of crayons to keep the youngsters busy coloring a surfboarding crocodile while they're waiting for their meals.

Toss (702/451-8677) specializes in "tossed" as opposed to stir-fried dishes. Menu items include Thai pan noodles, lo mein, curry chicken, catfish in black bean sauce, kung pao shrimp, and about a hundred other items. The kid's menu offers the choice of a mini-teriyaki chicken bowl with beverage or mini-ninja chicken nuggets and cream cheese wonton with soda or ice tea.

Viva Mercado's Mexican Restaurant & Cantina (702/735-6325, also at 6182 W. Flamingo Road; 702/871-8826) has 110 menu choices, including some that aren't often found this side of the border. There are *jalitos* (jalapeño peppers stuffed with cheddar cheese and covered with batter); *camarones al mojo de aho* (white shrimp sauteed in garlic, white wine, and orange juice); and *enchiladas de calabacitas en tomatillo* (corn tortillas filled with baby zucchini, spinach, mushrooms, and onions simmered in a tomatillo sauce). You can also build your own quesadilla, priced according to the numbers of items (chicken, beef, green chiles, shrimp, guacamole, sour cream) you choose to add to the cheese.

Though there's a microbrewery at **Barley's Brew House** (702/458-2739) and it includes a gaming area, children are allowed to eat in the restaurant as well as outside. They're also allowed to tour the microbrewery (tours must be requested in advance). On the menu are a trio of burgers, a build-your-own pizza, and a sourdough bread bowl filled with Barley's signature beef-barley soup. Sandwiches include Brew Pub Bratwurst, Barley's Philadelphia (thinly sliced sirloin or chicken with mushrooms, onions, and bell pepper, topped with melted Swiss cheese), and sesame-encrusted orange roughy. Among dinner entrees are a mixed grill of marinated chicken breast, baby back ribs, and shrimp at the high end of the price range and tavern fish and french fries at the low end.

For people who need even more choices, there's also **Swensen's**, with its wide selection of sandwiches and ice cream treats.

Prices at all the restaurants around the courtyard are moderate. Incidentally, this Green Valley Center food court is one of the favorite eating spots for families that live in Las Vegas and Henderson.

Casual Dining

Bakeries are great places to find just the right food for hotel-room breakfasts. At the **Diamond Bakery** (Chinatown Plaza, 4255 Spring Mountain Road; 702/221-8448), counters brim with such delights as kiwi mango and peach mousse cakes, coconut bread, red bean toast, and a variety of buns (try the lotus buns for breakfast; the onion and bacon if it's lunchtime). An added treat is the display of wedding cakes and cake decorations near the entrance.

Freed's (4780 S. Eastern Avenue; 702/456-7762) isn't fancy. Stacks of plastic-windowed boxes containing wedding-cake decorations on the shelves; a couple of Formica tables, and chairs for customers who can't wait to eat the goodies they've bought provide the ambience. And the counters brim with such delights as Hungarian cheesecake, poppy seed strudel, French pastries, and honey-pecan bars called *Bienenstich* that have kept Las Vegans coming back for two or three generations.

Picnics the Kids Won't Soon Forget

- Buy a one- or two-foot long submarine sandwich with your favorite fillings at **Port of Subs** (2285 W. Green Valley Parkway, 2601 Windmill Parkway, and 1405 W. Sunset Road) or **Blimpie** (2600 W. Sahara and 1146 W. Sunset), soft drinks, and a toy sailboat for each child. Then go to Sunset Park at the corner of Sunset and Eastern. It's a huge park—324.5 acres—with plenty of running room and a pond for sailing the boats. Since it's also a great place for watching the planes coming in to land at McCarran International Airport, you may want to bring along balsa wood gliders instead.

- Pack an assortment of fruit, cream cheese, and other spreads from the supermarket, plus a selection of bagels from **Harry's Bagelmania** (855 W. Twain Avenue) and eat your lunch while you take in a free noontime concert at Clark County Government Center Amphitheater downtown or a summer evening jazz performance at Jaycee Park (corner of St. Louis and Eastern Avenues).

- Bring Chinese take-out in cartons and a stack of paper plates from **Panda Express** (numerous locations including 3480 S. Maryland Parkway, No. 10; 702/737-1616) or **Pick Up Stix** (2101 N. Rainbow Boulevard, No. 100; 702/636-6600) for an alfresco meal at Foxridge, a quiet little neighborhood park at the corner of Valle Verde and Foxridge Drive in Henderson. (*One word of caution:* When visiting any Las Vegas park on very warm days, be sure to check out the playground equipment before the children start to play. If the swings, merry-go-rounds, or slides are made of metal, they'll be sizzling hot to the touch.)

- Choose your favorite kinds of sandwiches at **Celebrity Deli** (4055 S. Maryland Parkway at Flamingo) and have a strolling picnic as you meander along the walkways of the UNLV campus, which fronts on Maryland Parkway about five blocks south. If you pass by the Thomas & Mack Center at the southwest edge of the campus on an autumn afternoon, you may see the Running Rebel football team practicing or the band rehearsing an upcoming half-time routine.

- Get a big pizza or calzone at **Bootleggers** (Village East Plaza, 5025 Eastern Avenue) and have an Italian picnic at Winchester Park (3130 S. McLeod Drive). After you've eaten, wander over to the bocce ball court and watch the action. You will also find a horseshoe pit, shuffleboard, as well as tennis and volleyball courts at this ten-acre park.

- Drive to the vista point at Red Rock Canyon (see chapter 10) for a breakfast picnic (bring along pastries from any of the bakeries listed previously, juice, and anything else that strikes the family's fancy). If you can't make it in early morning, change the menu and try for just before sunset.

- Order hot dogs at **Nathan's Famous** (3799 Las Vegas Boulevard S.) and bring them to Dog Fancier's/Horsemen's Park (5800 E. Flamingo Road; 702/455-7509) on a day when a dog show or gymkhana is taking place.

- Go to any supermarket you happen to see and let each person in your party choose one item for the picnic (it's vacation, remember, so don't worry about balanced meals). Head for **Arroyo Grande Sports Complex** (298 Arroyo Grande, Henderson) where there's almost always a little league, softball, or baseball game to watch on summer evenings.

Families committed to healthful eating even when they're on vacation will want to have lunch at **Wild Oats Community Market** (6720 W. Sahara; 702/253-7050). Shakes made with non-fat frozen yogurt and skim milk, vegetarian pasta with wheat balls, and all sorts of imaginative sandwiches will convince you that eating what's good for you is anything but ho hum.

Bargain Dining

If money's tight, Las Vegas is a good place to find cheap—and even free—eats. The best hot dogs in town are given away at **Lady Luck Casino** (206 N. Third Street; 702/477-3000). Coupons for the hot dogs are part of the Lady Luck funpack, which you receive by presenting the ad found in several of the free weekly/monthly entertainment magazines and also selected airline in-flight magazines. The hot dogs are huge—big enough for two people. Several two-for-one food offers are included in the Flamingo Hilton funpack—two hamburgers for the price of one, the second ice cream cone free—and you'll find several other free food or snack offers in the entertainment magazines. If you're the only adult in your party, it's difficult to take advantage of the offers that you have to walk through the casino to get. Several offers, however, such as those at the neighborhood Texas Casino, are available in the food area, which is not restricted to adults.

The prize for the very cheapest casino meals has to go to the Holiday Inn/Boardwalk. Throughout the year it offers a variety of specials, such as three burgers for $1.29.

Teenagers may want to stay up for the "graveyard specials," usually served at casino restaurants from 11:00 P.M. to 5:00 or 6:00 A.M. The food ranges from New York strip steaks with salad, baked potato, and rolls to big country-style breakfasts—eggs, ham, bacon or sausage, hash browns, and toast—at bargain prices (for example, it is possible to get a steak and eggs breakfast for less than $3). These specials are usually announced on the casinos' marquees.

One of the best ways to economize on food is by buying fruit, breakfast food, and milk at the supermarket (keep the milk on ice in the bucket in your hotel room if you haven't brought an ice chest along in the car). Buy the makings for picnic lunches and even dinners at the market, too. One that's convenient to the Strip is **Myer's Market** (22 W. Oakey Boulevard; 702/369-3322). It's more expensive than the supermarket chains, but works well if you don't have a car. The leading chains are Albertson's Food & Drug Stores, Lucky Food Centers, Smith's Food and Drug Centers, and Vons. Each of them has more than a dozen locations throughout the city.

I realize that some children won't think their vacation is all it should be without at least once in a while having a McDonald's Happy Meal, a Frosty from Wendy's, or a Taco Bell taco. So here are the addresses of those most conveniently located to the Strip and Glitter Gulch. Prices, however, may be less expensive at those franchises located away from the tourist areas.

- McDonald's is located in the Monte Carlo Hotel, in Fitzgeralds/Holiday Inn (301 Fremont Avenue), and at 300 N. Casino Center Boulevard.
- Wendy's locations tend to be in more outlying areas of the city, but those most convenient to tourists will probably be the restaurants at 3333 W. Tropicana, 4780 S. Maryland Parkway, and 2510 E. Tropicana.
- Among the nearest Taco Bells are those at 3055 Las Vegas Boulevard S., 2295 E. Tropicana Avenue, and 4030 S. Maryland Parkway.

Whether you prefer fast food or leisurely meals, there are occasions when Mom's feet hurt, Dad's tired of telling people to behave, everyone's hungry, and what the kids need most is some cooling-off time. That's when—whatever the family vacation budget—you'll say, "Thank heaven for room service."

CHAPTER 4

Transportation Tips

Some cities, even those where millions of people live, are small enough geographically that you can get almost anywhere you want to go without resorting to mechanized transportation. But Las Vegas is not one of them. A sprawl of a city, it keeps on growing at a pace faster than any other U.S. metropolitan area. Each year, dozens of subdivisions, business establishments, and attractions spring up on the city's periphery. In fact, southeast of the city's center, you cannot tell whether you're in Las Vegas or Henderson, which was ten miles away a few years ago. Fortunately, you have a choice of several modes of travel to get from one place to another.

Transportation

The first transportation you'll need if you arrive in Las Vegas by air will be to take you from the airport to your hotel or motel. Since few hotels have their own shuttle service, you have to take public transportation unless you rent a car.

A taxi will cost you $7.50 to $10.00 to the south Strip (Excalibur, Luxor, Tropicana, San Remo, MGM Grand, New York-New York, and other lodging places in that area); $9 to $12 to the center Strip (Flamingo Hilton, Mirage, Treasure Island, Caesars Palace and neighboring properties); $12 to $13 to the north Strip (Riviera, Stardust, Frontier, Westward Ho, Circus Circus, and Stratosphere); and $14 to $16 to downtown.

Two companies, Bell Trans (702/385-5466) and Gray Line (702/739-5700), are the most prominent companies at the airport for van and limousine service to the major hotels. Both van and limousine cost the same, $3.50 per person to the Strip and $4.75 to downtown. The limos are far more comfortable than the shuttles, which are short on leg room and often seem to need their shock absorbers replaced. You can't choose which one you want, however, and have to take whatever kind of vehicle is waiting at the pickup zone when you're ready to go.

Limousine service is also available on an hourly basis, ranging from $33 to $42 an hour. Stretch limos' hourly rates are $60 to $65. Among the more than a dozen licensed limousine services in addition to Bell Trans and Gray Line are:

LV Limo	702/739-8414
CLS Las Vegas	702/740-4545
On Demand Sedan	702/876-2222
Presidential Limo	702/731-5577

Driving Your Own Car

If you've arrived in Las Vegas via automobile, aside from incessant traffic on the Strip, your transportation problems are solved. Properties along the Strip, as well as off-Strip hotel/casinos, have free parking in adjacent multistory parking garages. Time was when you could park outside in large lots, but real estate on the Strip and downtown has become so valuable that that's no longer the case. As a result, the walk from the garage to the hotel can be a long one.

Happily, all the big hotel/casinos have valet parking, which is also free (it's customary, however, to tip $1 or $2 when your car is brought to you). Valet service is usually prompt, but at afternoon check-in time (2:00 P.M. to 4:00 P.M), you may have to wait a while. The disadvantage of the valet parking system is that you don't have easy access to your car if you've left items that you need in it. One solution is to drop the family and luggage off at the hotel entrance, then park the car yourself in the garage.

Driving in Las Vegas is fairly straightforward. The city is essentially laid out on a north-south/east-west grid, although four principal thoroughfares—U.S. 95 (a freeway running through town); Fremont Street (which becomes Boulder Highway and joins U.S. 95 a few miles out of town); Rancho Boulevard; and part of Las Vegas Boulevard—run diagonally. Major streets such as Tropicana Avenue, Flamingo Road, Desert Inn Road, Sahara Avenue, and Charleston Boulevard run east/west. Paradise Road, Maryland Parkway, Eastern Avenue, Valley View Boulevard, and Decatur Boulevard run north/south.

Only one of the city's major thoroughfares is confusing. That's Spring Mountain Road, which changes its name to Sands Avenue when it crosses Las Vegas Boulevard South and then after a short distance becomes Twain Avenue. Streets are broad and traffic is stop/start only during rush hours (except on the Strip, where it's often horrendous from before noon until after midnight). Be prepared during non-rush hours to drive above the posted speed limit if you're determined to keep up with the flow of traffic.

Other Ways to Get Around

The extensive Citizens Area Transit (CAT) bus system, with approximately thirty different routes, goes almost everywhere in the Las Vegas area. It's especially valuable when you want to go from one place on the Strip to another or between the Strip and downtown. The Strip buses cost $2.00, while fare for residential routes is $1.25; children from five to seventeen, seniors with cards issued by CAT, and the disabled ride for $1.00 on the Strip buses and $.60 on the other routes (exact change required).

Transfers are free. If you anticipate riding buses on several occasions, buy a bag of 40 tokens (called CAT coins), to save a little money and a good deal of hassle searching for exact change. Buses run along the Strip twenty-four hours every day and from 5:00 A.M. until 1:00 A.M. on residential routes.

Some of the buses that run to and from downtown along the Strip to Vacation Village are timed so that connections can be made with free shuttle service to Belz Outlet Mall and the Las Vegas Factory Stores. Vacation Village is also the transfer point for several other bus routes, including route 212, which goes past Sunset Park and the Ethel M. Chocolate Factory. Buses are also a great way to see the nontourist areas of the city if you aren't pressed for time. They're generally least crowded during the middle part of the day.

On your first ride, grab a "System Map and Guide to Services" and the "Time Schedule and Map Book" from a rack at the front of the bus. The former features a large, easy-to-understand map of all the routes plus fare information. The latter devotes two pages, including a small map, to each individual route. You can also obtain these publications in advance by writing CAT (see chapter 11).

Trolleys, Shuttles, Trams, and a Monorail

In addition to the CAT buses, trolleys go up and down the Strip, stopping at each of the major hotel/casinos along the way. Trolley fare is $1.50 along the Strip, with an additional $1.50 from the Stratosphere to downtown. Although not having to walk to the nearest bus stop is an advantage for people staying at major hotels, the ride is rougher and service is not quite so frequent.

There is also a downtown trolley, which goes down Fremont, Main, Stewart, and Ogden Streets and costs $.50 for adults and $.25 for children and seniors (exact change). The trolley operates daily except on Thanksgiving, Christmas, and New Year's Day from 7:30 A.M. to 11:00 P.M.

Several hotel/casinos offer transportation to other properties. For example, you can take these free shuttles between the California Hotel in Glitter Gulch and Sam's Town on the Boulder Highway and the Stardust on the Strip. Others go between the Barbary Coast, Gold Coast, Polo Towers, and Stratosphere; the Rio Suite Hotel and Casino, MGM Grand, and the Forum Shops; and Fashion Show Mall, MGM Grand, Boulder Station, Palace Station, Fiesta, Boomtown, and Hard Rock.

The MGM-Bally's monorail consists of two 6-car trains on a one-mile, dual-lane gridway. Powered by electricity, the twenty-two-foot-high elevated monorail parallels the Las Vegas Strip on Audrie Street. The air conditioned trains, which can transport a thousand passengers per hour, make the trip and load and unload passengers in three and a half minutes. Entrances are near MGM Grand's port cochere entrance and at Bally's on Audrie Street. Construction for extension of the monorail to Sahara Avenue, scheduled to begin in 2002, will not be completed for several years.

Trams run between Luxor/Excalibur and Mirage/Treasure Island. They don't save a great deal of walking, however, since it's quite a distance from the Strip to the casino entrances and then you must proceed through the casinos in some cases to get to the tram stations.

Taxis

A dozen or more different taxi companies operate in the Las Vegas metro area. The basic taxi fare, controlled by the Nevada Taxicab Authority, is $2.20 for the first mile and $1.50 for each additional mile, with a five-passenger maximum. But time also ticks away on taxi meters. When taxis are stopped at red lights, the charge is $.35 a minute; you may pay a great deal more than the posted rates. A ride from one end of the three-and-a-half-mile Strip to the other can cost you $20 when Las Vegas Boulevard South is in gridlock.

Any time you take a cab, tell the driver specifically that you want to go by the least expensive rather than the shortest route. Often the shortest route, which taxi drivers are required to use unless instructed otherwise, can cost twice as much as a route along streets unclogged by traffic.

Your best places to get taxis quickly are the main entrances to any of the major hotel/casinos. Hailing a cab is almost impossible during rush hours, Friday afternoons, or when large conventions/trade shows are in town.

Major cab companies include:

ABC Union Cab Co.	702/736-8444
Ace Cab Co.	702/736-8383
Checker Cab Co.	702/873-2000
Desert Cab Co.	702/386-9102
Henderson Taxi	702/384-2322
Star Cab Co.	702/873-2000
Whittlesea Blue Cab	702/384-6111
Yellow Cab Co.	702/873-2000

Even though you rely primarily on public transportation, sometime during your Las Vegas stay, you'll probably want to rent a car if you don't already have one at your disposal. Major rental agencies, most of which have toll-free numbers, include:

Airport Rent a Car	702/893-3791
Alamo	800/327-9633
Allstate Car Rental	800/634-6186
Avis Rent A Car	800/831-2847
Budget Car & Truck Rental	800/527-0700
Dollar Rent-A-Car	800/800-4000
Enterprise Rent-A-Car	800/325-8007

Hertz	800/654-3131
National Car Rental	800/CAR-RENT
Payless Car Rental	800/PAYLESS
Rent-A-Vette	800/372-1981
Sav-mor	702/736-1234
Sunbelt	702/731-3600
Thrifty Car Rental	800/367-2277

The cost of car rentals can vary so widely—not only from season to season, but also from one rental agency to another—that it pays to shop around. When the town is loaded with fly-in visitors, rental prices rise with the demand.

Ask a number of questions when you're phoning the agencies: How far in advance must I make a reservation? (It's often twenty-four hours.) Are there charges for additional drivers? Do drop-off charges apply if I want to pick the car up at my hotel and turn it in at the airport? Some agencies give unlimited mileage only to California, Nevada, and Arizona residents. And there are companies that charge an additional fee when customers arrive at the agency offices via airport shuttle.

Allow plenty of time for picking up your car. Lines from out of the rental agencies into the parking lots are not uncommon. Also, remember to have an attendant mark down any damage you have noted on the car *prior* to your leaving the agency lot. Then check to see if what the attendant has written agrees with what you have observed. You may get a bit of static from some attendants, but the extra time you take will be well worth it. Also, never leave anything of value in the car trunk, because keys for the same make of car are often identical—and easy to obtain.

Bike Hiking

Your family may be one that enjoys bicycling together. Though there are few bike paths in Las Vegas, you'll find that riding along streets in quiet residential neighborhoods and on day trips out of town (see chapter 10) is safe and enjoyable—but be sure to take along your water bottles.

If you haven't brought your bikes with you, you can rent them at several locations in the city. Rentals (which usually include helmets, water bottle holders, and saddle bags) are in the $25- to $45-a-day range, depending upon the kind of bicycle you want. You won't want to ride along the major Las Vegas streets, as there's simply too much traffic, but there are lots of residential areas, especially in the southeast part of the city, that make for enjoyable bicycling.

Las Vegas Walk-About

Though Las Vegas covers an enormous area, it is flat as a city can be, and many of its attractions are within easy walking distance of one another. As a result, families that like to hike together will have plenty of opportunities to do so.

Because some of those walking distances are fairly long, persuade children who think they're too big for strollers to push favorite stuffed toys or dolls in them. Chances are they won't fuss about climbing in themselves when they're sufficiently tired.

Don't forget that though tropical flowers bloom and palm trees sway, before the advent of irrigation, Las Vegas was a desert. Humidity is generally less than most visitors are accustomed to; therefore, you and your family probably won't be conscious of how much liquid your bodies are losing. It's important that everyone drinks plenty of fluids, especially during summer. And since almost three hundred days of the year are sunny, sunscreen and sun hats are a good idea.

Las Vegas, with its large transient population, is like any other metropolitan area where there are places you really ought not to go walking through due to the high probability of crime. Among them are the Lied Children's Discovery Museum/Museum of Natural History/Cashman Field area on Las Vegas Boulevard N. and around Sunrise Medical Center and Boulevard Mall on S.

Maryland Parkway.

The Strip, however, is considered to be safe twenty-four hours a day, especially if you take customary precautions such as carrying wallets in inside pockets and holding purses securely (or better yet, not carrying them). It's safer, too, to leave valuable jewelry in a secure place rather than wearing it.

Whether you walk or ride around Las Vegas, you'll want to have a good map. Finding one that's up-to-date is tough since the city is growing so rapidly. Most attractions are in well-established areas, however, so if a map was published in the last few years it should work for you. One of the easiest maps to read (the print is big) is the free CAT bus route map.

CHAPTER 5

Shopping Sprees

Shopping, it has been said, is America's second most popular recreational pasttime, surpassed only by watching TV. I wouldn't swear that's true, but I do know that people who like to shop don't stop shopping because they're on vacation.

In fact, it's usually more interesting to browse around stores with which you're not familiar than it is to shop at home. And even if you visited Las Vegas six months ago, you'll find new businesses galore. For in addition to the thousands of stores that have been around for a while, new ones open every week.

Because of the city's tremendous tourist count, the number of places to buy things is way out of proportion to its population size. You will find upscale shopping arcades in the major hotels, sleezy souvenir shops on the Strip between casinos, mega-malls, factory outlets, an antiques mall, and neighborhood shopping centers. You can buy everything from miniature slot machines to kiddies' designer clothes; environmentally sensitive items to those covered with sequins and spangles that won't biodegrade in a thousand years; and just about everything in between.

Mall Cruising

Boulevard Mall is located five minutes east of the Strip on Maryland Parkway South between Desert Inn Road and Twain (702/735-8268; eastbound bus 203 from Fashion Show Mall on the Strip to Maryland Parkway South). Boulevard Mall's anchors are J.C. Penney's, Dillard's, the Broadway, and Sears. Sesame Street General Store, Nature Company, and Bombay Company are among the more interesting of the 123 stores in the complex.

Meadows Mall, two miles west of downtown at the intersection of U.S. 95 and Valley View (702/878-4849) has department stores from the same chains as Boulevard, and is twenty or so stores larger. (To get to the mall from the Strip, take westbound bus 203 from Fashion Show Mall to Valley View; then northbound bus 104 to the mall.)

The **Galleria at Sunset** (1300 W. Sunset Road, Henderson; 702/434-2409) is the newest mega-mall in the Las Vegas orbit. With some 110 stores, its anchors are Dillards, J.C. Penney's, Robinsons-May, and Mervyns. Mall decor is Southwest, with muted colors and an array of fountains that give shoppers a feeling of oasis even on the hottest days. Its shops include Gap Kids/Baby Gap, Flapdoodles, and Gymboree for youngsters' clothes plus several teenagers' favorites.

Special events are presented regularly on the eastern end of the mall's lower level, which are announced on free-standing signs at all the shopping centers' entrances. Among those that the children enjoy most are the Magic School Bus/Lied Discovery Children's Museum/KLVX-TV-sponsored presentations, which feature hands-on science, look-alike contests, and other well-planned activities. To get to Galleria at Sunset by public transportation, take bus 202 from Vacation Village at the south end of the Strip.

Belz Factory Outlet World, at 7400 Las Vegas Boulevard S. (702/896-5599), is fully enclosed and climate-controlled, and presents a state-of-the-art laser show every hour on the domed ceiling in front of the food court. It's also the only nonsmoking shopping facility in Nevada. Besides all that, of course, there are more than 145 stores. This is the place to go if you have young children and are looking for bargains. The big Buster Brown, Carter's, Baby OshKosh, and Danskin outlet prices are normally about one-third off retail, but often have special racks with clothing marked at 40 to 50 percent off. Publishers Warehouse carries children's books that sell for 50 percent off list price. Another deal gives 20 percent off any book that sells for $3.99 or more when you buy three books. At Toy Liquidators, Barbie dolls sell from one-fourth to one-third off retail. Though Belz doesn't have many stores specifically aimed at preteens and teenagers, there are two they especially like—Rue 21 and Esprit.

One of the latest additions to the discount shopping scene is the **Off Fifth Saks Fifth Avenue Outlet** (702/263-7692), housed in a free-standing building across the parking lot from the Belz Factory Outlet World's main buildings. Carrying men's, women's, and children's clothes, as well as an upscale selection of houseware, the outlet's selections are good and prices are 40 to 70 percent off original retail. In September, summer clothes—including those with Donna Karan, Calvin Klein, and other top designers' labels—sell at up to 60 percent off the discounted prices (on one trip I bought three designer swimsuits for a total of $45). An especially good time to shop any of the outlet stores is at the end of summer, when the discounted merchandise is marked down even farther. A free shuttle goes from Vacation Village to the outlet complex.

The state's most upscale outlet mall is about a half-hour's drive southwest of Las Vegas on the California state line at Primm/Stateline. You can get there even more quickly if you spend your savings in advance and take a helicopter.

Just Looking, Thank You

Shopping in Las Vegas can be exciting even if you don't plan to buy a thing. It can be entertaining, and at times, educational, to look at art objects that we have no desire to possess or intention of ever owning. And in Las Vegas there are lots of baubles, bangles, and the like for sale that are fun to look at even though they're well out of most of our price ranges.

Big spenders by the thousands visit Las Vegas on a daily basis; and a lot of wealthy people live in the city. Then there are those winners, who after hitting an $800 or $8,000 or $800,000 jackpot want to go out and spend their money. As a result, high-ticket items are the order of business in many of the casino arcade boutiques as well as at Fashion Show Mall and the Forum Shops on the Strip.

The Strip's new megaresorts—Aladdin, Bellagio, Mandalay Bay, Paris, and the Venetian—all have shopping arcades, ranging from a clutch of chichi boutiques at Via Bellagio to 130 shops and restaurants at Desert Passage, which joins Aladdin.

Desert Passage is the city's newest shopping hot spot. The architecture is Mediterranean/North African trade route/Las Vegas, with intricate mosaic tile floors, Moorish arches, filigreed entry ways, and other touches straight out of *Casablanca* and the French foreign legion films. Even the names of the areas within the complex—India Gate, Lost City, Merchant's Harbor—conjure up images of adventure. Every half hour, one of the world's few indoor rainstorms falls on a ship docked at Merchant's Harbor; acrobats, belly dancers, and other street performers entertain shoppers as they stroll along the walkways. Henna artists at the Morocco Gate entrance provide entertainment of another sort for the galleries of onlookers who watch as the artists paint intricate designs on their customers' skin. Rides in the gaily decorated, bicycle-drawn pedicabs are free, but their operators are dependent on tips for their incomes.

The most exciting way to approach the Grand Canal Shoppes

at the Venetian is by riding in a gondola to St. Mark's Square, then leisurely exploring the stores. Some of them, such as Ciao, Buon Giorno, and Ripa de Monte are Italian themed, but most are international in scope. One youngsters will especially enjoy is Toys International, which features toys from around the world (more on individual stores follows later in this chapter).

Ceasars Palace **Appian Way** (3570 Las Vegas Boulevard S.) features some of Las Vegas's most exclusive shops along an elegant promenade, and resort wear is a specialty at Mirage's **Esplanade** (3400 Las Vegas Boulevard S.). Flamingo Hilton, Riviera, Stardust, and Stratosphere are among the other hotels with arcade shops.

Fashion Show Mall, on the Strip between the Mirage and Frontier hotels (702/369-8382), is definitely upscale. Currently anchored by Dillard's, Robinsons-May, Nieman Marcus, and Saks Fifth Avenue, the mall is in the throes of a $350 million expansion. When completed in 2002, it will be home to four more anchor stores, including Bloomingdales and Nord-stroms, and the size of the center will double. There will be a center stage, too, for fashion shows and other entertainment.

Don't expect run-of-the-mill stores or surroundings at the **Forum Shops at Caesars** (3500 Las Vegas Boulevard S.; 702/893-4800) either. For one thing, the statues in its Great Roman Hall centerpiece talk. For another, the clouds and light of the domed ceiling provide a constantly changing sky overhead: one minute you are strolling under the morning sun, and a few minutes later, stars begin to twinkle. The entrance to this Roman streetscape—lined with luxury shops such as Gucci, Escada, Gianni Versace, and Louis Vuitton—is in Caesars Palace. It's worth the fairly long trek from the street and through the casino, even for confirmed nonshoppers (there's also underground valet parking at the Forum Shops' entrance).

The Roman portion of the complex was built in 1992. Five years later, it was doubled in size, with more shops, restaurants, and wonders added. Chances are, the store in the new addition that youngsters will like best is the world's largest FAO Schwartz. In fact, they'll be enchanted even before they go inside, for the store windows are filled with mechanized animals. One group is working in a ceramics factory—mixing clay, throwing pots, firing them in a kiln, and packing them in crates. Another scene is of stuffed bears wearing laurel wreaths and arranged as a Roman procession, complete with chariot. Even better than the window displays, however, is the huge Trojan horse at the store's entrance.

Centerpiece of this section of the Forum Shops is a circular monument containing a 50,000-gallon aquarium. Atop the monument is a statue of Poseidon, ruler of the mythical underwater kingdom of Atlantis, and in the aquarium swim rare species of fish brought to Las Vegas from the region of the Atlantic Ocean where it's conjectured that the lost city of Atlantis could have existed.

This attraction, in a city where most everything has a theme, ties into the free "Atlantis" spectacle that's presented every hour on the half-hour from 11:30 A.M. until closing (the statues in the Great Roman Hall do their stuff in a light, sound, and laser show every hour on the hour beginning at 11:00 A.M.). The Atlantis production features humans and animatronic figures in a battle between Atlas' son and daughter to gain power over the mythical underwater kingdom and is more interesting technologically than the Great Roman Hall show. Each show lasts approximately ten minutes.

If shopping at Saks Fifth Avenue, Nieman Marcus, and the Forum Shops ordinarily seems out of the economic question, consider catching one of their sales. According to two salespeople who have worked at Saks for several years, the store's best sales are from December 26 through the first of the New Year—furs especially, are a good buy. Those in the know at Nieman Marcus say that though it has both summer and winter "Last Call" sales, when all sale merchandise is marked down still farther, the sale that begins in mid-January is definitely the best. Savings, they say, can be as much as 60 percent.

Showcase, just north of MGM Grand on Las Vegas Boulevard South, is often referred to as a mall, but is actually an attractions center (see chapter 6). You can do some shopping there, however. Though much of the World of Coca-Cola attraction is no longer in operation, a large area is devoted to the retailing of Coke-related memorabilia—trays, neckties, pictures, Christmas tree ornaments, and other souvenir items.

Las Vegas stores generally open at 9:30 or 10:00 A.M. and remain open until 5:30 or 6:00 P.M. Most mall stores stay open until 9:00 P.M. except on Saturday and Sunday nights when they close earlier. Some Forum Shops stay open until 11:00 P.M.

Since Las Vegas is a twenty-four-hour town, however, you can buy most anything you need anytime—even in the middle of the night. Wal-Mart, with four Las Vegas locations, Sav-On Drugs (four locations also), and almost all grocery stores are among the stores open round the clock.

Specialty Shopping

Las Vegas is definitely the place to buy items that you most likely won't find anywhere else. Following are among the most interesting of the shops we've found.

Holy Cow! (2423 Las Vegas Boulevard S.; 702/732-2697) has a gift shop with nothing but "cowlectibles" for sale. Black-and-white Holstein-patterned napkins, coasters, bibs, boxer shorts, coffee mugs, and cream pitchers, plus an array of a hundred other bovine-themed items, are fun to look at even if they don't fit into your decorating schemes. And check out the Christmas tree ornaments. The cows in lace dresses are especially charming.

Shepler's (3025 E. Tropicana Avenue; 702/898-3000 and 4700 W. Sahara at Decatur; 702/258-2000) advertise themselves as the "World's Largest Western Stores." We don't know whether they are or not, but we do know they carry a huge selection of western wear—boots, belt buckles, bolo ties, and all. And speaking of boots, if you want to buy some at a bargain, Shepler's holds a "Thanksgiving Week Boot Blowout," with certain models marked down substantially. Shepler's advertisement, found in tourist brochure racks, is good for an extra 10 percent off regular and sale merchandise.

Ray's Beaver Bag (725 Las Vegas Boulevard S.; 702/386-8746) specializes, it would seem, in outfitting pioneers and mountain men. There are racks of gingham dresses and sunbonnets, coonskin caps, leather pouches and bags, and, of course, handmade mocassins. Frontier supplies include hunting knives and tomahawks, cast-iron skillets, and snake-tanning kits plus lots more. It's better than a good surplus store for browsing around.

Smokey's Baseball Card Shop (3734 Las Vegas Boulevard S.; 702/739-0003) is the largest card shop in Nevada, with baseball, football, basketball, and hockey memorabilia from 1910 to 1989 for sale. **Gallery of Legends** (Desert Passage; 702/866-0710) is another repository of sport star mementos such as autographs, pennants, posters, and sports cards.

If you would like to bring home a live cat or dog, you don't have to go to a pet shop. Animals available for adoption are shown on KLAS TV (Channel 8) every Tuesday morning between 7:45 and 8:00 A.M.

For educational toys that are fun, at the **Nature Company** (Boulevard Mall; 702/792-0877) you can buy all sorts of projects that the family can do together—birdhouse kits, science experiments, puzzles, or games. In fact, there are so many neat things in this store, you might be tempted to spend all your shopping time there. At **Lied Discovery Children's Museum** (833 Las Vegas Boulevard N.; 702/382-5437) and the **Las Vegas Natural History Museum** (900 Las Vegas Boulevard N.; 702/384-3466) gift shops, you'll also find a number of great educational toys and projects, as you will at the **Endangered Species Store** (Desert Passage).

Discovery Channel Stores at Desert Passage and the Forum Shops (both 702/866-0710) add another facet to Discovery Channel TV programming with hands-on games, experiments, and other materials focusing on nature, history, science, and technology. The stores are grand for nosing about, too, since they feature a variety of interactive exhibits as well as items for sale.

Children of all ages will enjoy designing their own personalized keepsakes at **Build-a-Bear Workshop** (Desert Passage; 702/866-0710). Plush bear bodies, stuffing machines, a multitude of clothes, and accessories are all available for purchase and assembly. If you pull out all the stops, the bears can cost a bunch, but they're charming.

Houdini's Magic Shop at the Venetian's Grand Canal Shoppes and the **Lance Burton Magic Shop** at Monte Carlo are places junior magicians won't want to miss. Not only are the tricks that are for sale out of the ordinary, but staff magicians are on hand to teach customers how to perform them.

The gift shop at **Madame Tussaud's Las Vegas Experience** (the Venetian) will produce all sorts of giggles and grins when the kids try on the wigs and glamour hats on display. And while **Toe Rings & Foot Things** (Boardwalk Casino, 3750 Las Vegas Boulevard S; 702/735-2400, ext. 3270) may not appeal to parents, teenagers will find that it's too cool. Along with more than two hundred styles of toe rings as well as foot beads and body jewelry, the store also carries Las Vegas charms. Ear piercing is available, too.

You may want to do some bookstore browsing, and if you do, you'll find that Las Vegas has many bookstores. I have found that the **Barnes & Noble** stores (2191 N. Rainbow Boulevard; 702/631-1775, and 567 N. Stephanie, Henderson; 702/434-1533) are among the most comfortable, with their upholstered chairs and friendly attitude toward browsers. There are also several used comic book stores, including **Silver Cactus Comics** (560 N. Nellis Boulevard; 702/438-4408) and **Kool Kollectables** (5197 W. Charleston Boulevard; 702/877-5665).

Ethnic Shopping Stops

One of the best ways to learn about other cultures is by looking at the products they use. In Las Vegas, due to its diverse ethnic population, there are several stores that specialize in imported products, primarily food. It's fascinating to look around **Gee's Oriental Market** (4109 E. Sahara Avenue; 702/362-5287) and **Asian Market** (935 E. Sahara; 702/734-7653), even if you don't buy the dried seaweed and preserved chicken legs. If your family likes Asian cooking, you'll be happy to find fish paste, lemon grass, chutneys, and other ingredients that aren't readily available in most supermarkets. The stores also carry rice steamers, woks, and inexpensive porcelain dishes for serving Oriental food.

At **Supermercado del Pueblo #2** (4972 S. Maryland Parkway; 702/891-0282), you'll see bakery cases with traditional Mexican pastries, cookies, and *empanadas*, as well as several products made in Mexico. The Gamesa brand ice cream wafers are especially delicious. In the produce department are imported Mexican limes, *limones*, which are usually difficult to find in the United States. **New India Sweets & Spices** (953 E. Sahara Avenue; 702/892-0720) carries Indian and Pakistani groceries; and **Fasika Ethiopian Restaurant & Mart** (860 E. Twain Avenue; 702/699-7042) sells spices used in Ethiopian cookery.

While the emphasis at **Cost Plus World Market** (3840 S. Maryland Parkway; 702/794-2070) is on furniture and housewares from around the globe, many of the items, such as out-of-the-ordinary napkin rings, gift wrap, and toys, will interest the children.

Alternative Shopping

You won't be in Las Vegas long before you notice the pawn-shops in Glitter Gulch and along the Strip. Much of their merchandise comes from gamblers who hock their watches or walkmans or blowtorches for a little more gambling money and never redeem the pledged items. But pawnshops get their merchandise from other sources, too. They may buy remaining stock from retail stores going out of business or from fire sales. Other items come from stores that take used goods, such as cameras and stereo equipment, on trade. And yes, it's possible that stolen goods pass over some of their counters, though the police department's pawnshop detail works hard to prevent this from happening.

Even if you don't plan on buying anything, Las Vegas pawn-shops are intriguing to browse around. The array of items can be pretty incredible—everything from guitars hanging from the ceilings and trays of flashy diamond rings to battery cables, chain saws, and exercise equipment.

If you do plan to make any pawn shop purchases, it's essential to know the going prices for items you want to buy. For example, a pawnshop sortie found that an identical model single-lens reflex camera was marked at various prices from $100 to $265, and the price for the same model in the used equipment department of a local camera store was $175.

Among the pawnshops that are fun to look around are **Ace Loan Company** (215 N. Third Street; 702/384-5771) and those located north and south of Fremont Street on First Street. Located there is one of the oldest. **Stoney's Super Pawn** (126 S. First Street; 702/384-0819) is the largest operation in town, with twelve locations. If you want to make a purchase at any of them, don't accept the first price you're quoted. Maybe not the second or third either.

Las Vegas has so many antique shops that the dyed-in-the-past collector could well spend an entire vacation poking about their nooks and crannies. Take your kids, however, only if they're able to look without touching, since most shops have a "break it and you've bought it" policy.

Antique Square (2014–2026 E. Charleston Boulevard) makes the job a little easier logistically. A dozen different shops make up the complex. **Nicholas & Osvaldo** (702/386-0238) is perhaps the most impressive of the group, and **Sweet D's** (702/386-8030) will probably have the biggest appeal with retro girls. A dozen or more other antiques and collectibles shops are concentrated in the same area on East Charleston Boulevard approximately two miles from downtown.

Garage sale addicts won't want to miss what's billed as "the biggest swap meet in Nevada," **Fantastic Indoor Swap Meet** (Decatur Boulevard at West Oakey; 702/877-0087), held on Friday, Saturday, and Sunday each week. More than one hundred vendors take part in the giant cut-rate shopping expo, selling everything from baseball cards to xylophones; motor oil to Elvis on black velvet. Admission for people over the age of twelve is $1; however, two-for-one admission coupons are widely circulated.

Among Your Souvenirs

My vote for best Las Vegas souvenirs that will undoubtedly become family keepsakes are pictures taken of your family in medieval costumes at **Castle Cameos,** the photo concession on the second floor of Excalibur. You can get a single 11-by-14-inch photo or one 8-by-10 and two 5-by-7 photos of two people (there's an extra charge for each additional person). One of the larger packages includes one 8-by-10, one 5-by-7, and eight wallet-size pictures. At the magazine concession, also on the second floor, you can have your framed photo on the cover of a magazine or on a T-shirt. Another magazine cover photo concession is Cashman Photo Magic at Desert Passage, where camera equipment and film are also for sale.

Other great Las Vegas souvenirs are the jigsaw puzzles that when put together become cartoon maps of Las Vegas or photos of the Strip and other attractions. You'll find the puzzles in gift shops and some drug stores as well.

You'll find thousands of souvenir possibilities at the multitude of logo shops in town. Among the most useful and attractive are those at the shop in the Hard Rock Hotel—really good-looking leather backpacks, snazzy aloha shirts, and alarm clocks are among the items that are a cut above the merchandise in most establishments of this sort.

Mirage Kidz Store on the Esplanade at Mirage carries logo items with a Las Vegas flair, such as denim jackets decorated with sequins. At **Animal Crackers** at the Forum (702/796-0121), along with a great selection of dolls and stuffed dogs that wag their tails, are glitzy Las Vegas T-shirts for kids. Souvenirs that the youngsters will love but which won't last long—unless the kids refuse to wash—are the temporary tattoos that are for sale at Harley-Davidson's logo store.

For children who enjoy picture books, consider buying western- and southwestern-themed books by Nevada authors. *Gully-washer* by Joyce Rossi and *Cowboy Country* by Ann Herbert Scott are especially appealing. Older children and adults will enjoy the *Nevada Trivia Book* by Richard Moreno. In question-and-answer format, selections in the Las Vegas section include:

Q. What performer, frequently identified with Las Vegas, made a less-than-impressive debut at the New Frontier in 1956 and didn't perform there again for thirteen years?

A. Elvis Presley

Although there are several coffee table books with photos of Las Vegas, I haven't found one yet that I think does the city justice. Look around and maybe you will, since new Las Vegas books come out frequently to keep pace with the area's growth.

You might consider bringing home food products made in Nevada as souvenirs. **Mrs. Auld's Gourmet Foods,** including sweet 'n spicy pickles, plum preserves, and salsa, are beautifully packaged and taste great.

You'll find edible souvenirs, too, in **Ethel M's** gigantic candy store (Showcase Mall), such as 10.5 ounces of chocolate fudge packed in a box that resembles a deck of playing cards, milk chocolate coins packaged in containers that look like slot machines, and the twenty-nine-ounce "A Taste of Las Vegas" assortment of chocolates with a photo montage of the city's casinos on the box cover.

Though children can't stand around the gaming areas in casinos, they can browse all they want at the **Gambler's General Store** (800 S. Main Street; 702/382-9903). It's a big establishment with lots of floor space devoted to gambling paraphernalia such as pool, poker, and crap tables; antique slot machines and reproductions of them; watches with slot machines and playing cards on their faces (kings on the men's watches, queens on the women's). There are bins of poker chips, hundreds of decks of cards, thousands of dice, neckties decorated with royal flushes, and all sorts of things that kids find fascinating.

The mother of souvenir stands is the **Bonanza Gift & Souvenir Shop** (just south of Stratosphere), billed as the largest souvenir store in the world. In this case, quantity doesn't necessarily equate with quality—or taste. Which makes this the ideal place to go if you're in the market for something particularly tacky to bring home to friends, such as the toilet seats embellished with gambling symbols or the sparkly lucite clocks with dice marking the hours.

Show and Tell

Since kids love to collect things—and there are plenty of brochures, sample menus, and other items to collect in Las Vegas—the souvenirs they enjoy most may be the ones they make. Give each child who is old enough to press the button a disposable camera, an album with clear plastic pages, and a manila envelope for each day of your trip. Encourage them to put their treasures in the albums (or the appropriate envelopes if you have something else planned) at the end of each day. Have the film developed when you get home. Getting the kids to complete their albums may be a hassle, but they'll thank you for the memories when they're adults.

CHAPTER 6

Attractions and Events

Worried about the kids getting bored in Las Vegas? Not on your life. In addition to the casino attractions calculated to woo the family trade, you'll also find the kinds of attractions that any city of a million inhabitants generates for its resident population.

In fact, there are so many things for families to see and do in Las Vegas that we have divided them into four chapters— Attractions and Events; Activities; After dark Entertainment; and Reviewing the Shows.

Even then, space doesn't permit us to let you know about every single one of them. Therefore, the attractions, events, activities, entertainments, and shows highlighted in this chapter and the three that follow have been selected on the basis of quality and variety. Since families come from different places, literally and figuratively, what makes a hit with one won't necessarily suit another. So read around the activities and attractions that you're not interested in and concentrate on those you are.

Strolling the Strip

Since the casinos are the magnetic force that draws most people to Las Vegas, they're the places most visitors—including families—want to look at first. Although children are not allowed near gaming area slot machines and tables, they can pass through the casinos on their way to attractions and restaurants.

Exploring every attraction on the Strip would take more time than most visitors have, so we recommend a three-part odyssey, which includes hitting the most interesting spots that Las Vegas Boulevard has to offer. Each of the three tours should take about two and a half to three hours. If you decide to spend more than a few minutes at an attraction or redeem some of the food and attractions coupons (it usually works best if one adult does the redeeming while another remains with the children at a family-oriented attraction nearby), they may take longer. There's additional information on the attractions at several of the hotel/casinos mentioned in chapter 2.

Tour One: South Strip

Mandalay Bay is the starting point for this tour. You'll want to walk around the grounds, for although nonguests can't use the hotel's fantastic water complex (see chapter 2), you will be able to catch glimpses of it from the pathways. Inside, don't miss the Shark Reef (described later in this chapter), the House of Blues with its collection of American folk art, or the lobby, where talking birds in huge cages call to passersby.

Up the boulevard, the Egyptian-themed **Luxor**'s pyramidal shapes and ten-story sphinx guarding the entrance look impressive from the air, but slightly hokey when viewed from the street. Nonetheless, the interior decor of the casino—in shades of burgundy, blue, and gold—sets it apart from other casinos, and its arcade and interactive experiences are among kids' Las Vegas favorites.

The two experiences—In Search of the Obelisk, Episode I and Episode II—should be seen in sequence. The Luxor Museum is billed to be an authentic replica of King Tut's tomb and contains Egyptian artifacts. From Luxor, take the free monorail to its next-door neighbor, **Excalibur,** and head for the lower level with plenty of change in your pockets. There you'll find the standard midway games and scams in medieval guise, as well as Magic Motion Simulator thrill ride. Kids also like the second floor, with its strolling entertainers, caricaturists, and concession stands.

Across the street to the east, you might want to check out the Amazon parrots, Moluccan cockatoos, toucans, flamingos, African crowned cranes, koi fish, and pygmy marmosets, the world's smallest monkeys. They reside along the Water Walk (a glass-enclosed moving sidewalk overlooking the water park) and in the gardens of the **Tropicana.** The Trop also presents a twelve-minute laser light show (in its garden area) each evening.

North of the Tropicana and across the street stands **MGM Grand Resort.** The MGM Grand Adventures theme park, much diminished from its former size, is now open only for private functions. However, inside the MGM Grand, you'll find the Lion Habitat—one of the best free attractions in town (described later in this chapter). Just north of MGM Grand are two attractions you won't want to miss: the giant Coca-Cola bottle shaped elevator and Gameworks, described later in this chapter. Also, the second floor of the Ethel M candy store, also in the showcase, is a retail store devoted to M&M's, where you'll find the candy-coated chocolates in twenty-one colors.

The next hotel/casino on the Strip is the new Arabian-themed **Aladdin,** which opened in summer, 2000. Adjacent to the hotel, Desert Passage is the city's newest shopping arcade (you will probably want to return later for a longer shopping session). Next door is another new hotel/casino, **Paris Las Vegas,** with a fifty-story replica of the Eiffel Tower. If it's a clear day, you might want to ride the elevator to the observation platform for a panoramic view of Las Vegas and the surrounding countryside. North of Paris, you'll come to **Bally's,** where kid-pleasing attractions include a games arcade and a charming ice cream parlor in the shopping arcade.

After crossing the street, admire Bellagio's Lake Bellagio and the re-created Italian village on its shores. You will probably want to return some evening after dark to see Bellagio's fountain show. It features more than 1,000 fountains that shoot water 240 feet in the air in a water ballet enhanced by special effects lighting and choreographed to musical favorites. After crossing the street, walk south past a strip mall (stop by at the tourist information/ticket office in the front if you're looking for brochures) to Holiday Inn/Boardwalk, home of the Dixie Dooley magic show (see chapter 9, Reviewing the Shows).

Next in line is the **Monte Carlo,** one of the Strip's newest hotel/casinos. Then it's **New York-New York,** where you'll definitely want to take a look around and the youngsters will cast longing glances at the roller coaster. Even though when first installed the roller coaster had some trouble with its braking system, there have been no reports of that problem lately. The façade of New York-New York offers its own rendition of the city's skyline, including the Statue of Liberty, Chrysler building, Brooklyn Bridge, and other historic landmarks. New York-New York is the logical place to end Tour One (you'll be about two blocks north of where the tour began).

Tour Two

First stop on Tour Two—**Treasure Island** (just south of the Las Vegas Boulevard S. and Spring Mountain Road intersection; 702/894-7111)—is one best made during late afternoon or early evening. At 4:00 P.M., 5:30 P.M., 7:00 P.M., 8:30 P.M., and 10:00 P.M. daily, except during windy or rainy weather, the best free entertainment in Las Vegas takes place on the moat outside the hotel/casino (aka Buccaneer Bay). Since the water battle between the pirate ship *Hispanola* and the British ship *Royal Britannia* is such a popular attraction, you'll want to arrive at least three quarters of an hour before performance time to get a good viewing spot. And so that you can view the water battle from both the pirate ship and the British sides of the gangway in front of the hotel/casino, you'll probably want to watch the spectacle twice—once at the beginning of this portion of your Strip stroll and again at its end. The performance begins when the British come upon the pirates unloading their booty. The battle that follows sounds and looks amazingly real. Pirates plunge from the masts into the waters below. Gunpowder explodes. Fire ignites the sails. And just as you think the pirates are sure to lose, they desperately fire one last cannonball and the *Royal Brittania* sinks below the water's surface.

People staying at Treasure Island soon learn that sipping soft drinks at a balcony table overlooking Buccaneer Bay (enter via the Battle Bar) will provide the kids with ringside seats to the British side of the spectacle. To get the best seats, it's necessary to get there forty-five minutes early.

After the performance, either visit Treasure Island's games arcade, go shopping at Fashion Show Mall, which is just to the north, or proceed south to the **Mirage Hotel & Casino,** one of Treasure Island's sister properties. Trams run between the two every four minutes.

At the Mirage, attraction options include the tiger habitat, the Secret Garden of Siegfried & Roy, the dolphin habitat, and games arcade, all described later in this chapter. Unless you visit after the sun goes down, you'll want to make a return at night in order to see its on-Strip attraction—a volcano that erupts every fifteen minutes from 7:00 P.M. until midnight.

South of the Mirage, the Forum Shops at Caesars offer a preview of the Roman theme that has made the adjacent **Caesars Palace** famous. Store facades you might find around Rome's Piazza Navona, Italian-style fountains, talking statues, and a domed ceiling that provides a constantly changing sky overhead make this a Las Vegas must-see. Your budget will determine whether you spend any money since shops and restaurants are among the most upscale in town (for more information see chapter 5).

Caesars Palace is primarily an adult destination, but its

grounds, complete with marble reproductions of classic statues, fountains, and imported cypress trees, are interesting for children to look at, too. Whether you conclude that the layout is awesome or corny/gauche (among the statues of Roman statesmen, philosophers, poets, and a charioteer is one of heavyweight champ Joe Louis), you'll agree that it's a one-of-a-kind.

Another seemingly incongruous landscape element is a replica on the north lawn of Thailand's popular Brahma shrine—one associated with good fortune and prosperity. But think about it for a minute and you'll realize that the quest for luck and prosperity is what Las Vegas is all about.

You approach Caesars via a moving sidewalk while Quo Vadis–like music plays in the background and a stately voice heralds the wonders inside the casino. Those wonders where youngsters are welcome include the games arcade and the hotel shops. Also part of Caesars is the Omnimax Theater, on which you'll find information later in this chapter.

At the intersection of Las Vegas Boulevard South and Flamingo Road (that's the same intersection where Tour One ended), cross Las Vegas Boulevard to **Barbary Coast**, best known for its stained-glass murals—one of them a clipper ship with billowing sails and the other an enchanted forest. The next hotel/casino is the Flamingo Hilton, and then it's the **Imperial Palace,** whose car collection is described later in this chapter.

Between the Imperial Palace and Harrah's, a cobblestone street bordered by New Orleans French Quarter–style buildings with wrought-iron balconies is a great place to catch your breath before continuing on to the **Venetian,** which was completed in 1999. Themed around Italy's most romantic city, the hotel/casino's replications of the Grand Canal, Rialto Bridge, Library Building, and St. Mark's Square aren't totally authentic, but have a joyful quality that makes them special. Three major attractions—Madame Tussaud's Celebrity Encounter (described later in this chapter), the Guggenheim Las Vegas Museum, and the Guggenheim–St. Petersburg Museum are located within the

Venetian's buildings. Younger children may not be interested in the latter two museums, but people of all ages will recognize at least some of the wax figures at Madame Tussaud's. After you've finished exploring the Venetian, take the pedestrian overcrossing to return to Treasure Island up the block and across the street for another look at the pirate battle.

Tour Three: North Strip and Beyond

There are only four major points of interest on Tour Three, but each of them is unusual, and the starting point, **Circus Circus,** is worth a special trip even if you don't want to see the rest. Circus Circus was the first family-themed hotel/casino in Las Vegas. The big draw, in addition to Grand Slam Canyon described in chapter 2, is the midway. While the "throwing darts at balloons" type of games are typical carny, the circus acts are as professional as you'll see anywhere. Performers—especially those with children—consider Circus Circus jobs among the best in the world since they don't have to keep moving around in order to make a living. As a result, the aerialists, unicyclists, animal acts, and clowns are top-notch. Performances begin on the hour from 11:00 A.M. until midnight.

The exhibits at **Guinness World of Records Museum** (2780 Las Vegas Boulevard S.; 702/792-3766) include the world's largest vegetables, the smallest animals, and many more. In the Amazing Humans section, a figure representing Krystyne Kolorful, the world's most tattooed lady, is one of the most unusual exhibits. Though it's not one of my favorites, kids, as well as adults who go for graphically illustrated trivia, seem to enjoy the museum. Discount coupons that apply toward the admission price ($4.95, adults; $3.95, seniors, students, and military; $2.95, children five to twelve) are widely distributed.

North of the Strip, which technically ends at the Sahara Hotel/ Casino, is **Holy Cow!** (2423 Las Vegas Boulevard S.; 702/732-2697), a bovine-themed restaurant, bar, and microbrewery mentioned in chapters 3 and 5. Not only is the building's exterior something to write home about, it also contains a gift shop filled with "cowlectibles" that are interesting even if you haven't the slightest intention of buying a cow-shaped pitcher or a backpack with black-and-white Holstein markings.

Fourth stop on the tour is **Stratosphere** (2000 Las Vegas Boulevard S.; 702/380-7777), an undeniably unique structure that rises 1,149 feet into the sky; America's tallest freestanding observation tower. Daredevils in your group will probably beg to go on the Stratosphere's High Roller (billed as the world's highest roller coaster) and Space Shot, which shoots riders 160 feet straight up the tower and lets them free-fall back. Since they opened for business, the rides have occasionally had mechanical difficulties, which convinces me that I wouldn't let my kids ride on them. The Stratosphere Tower, however, with indoor and outdoor observation decks that provide 360-degree views of Las Vegas and surroundings, is operational weekdays from 9:00 A.M. to 1:00 A.M. (2:00 A.M. on Fridays and Saturdays). Admission is $6 for adults ($3 with Nevada ID) and $3 for children four to twelve years old.

Stratosphere and Holy Cow! are quite a walk north of most of the Strip's attractions, so if there are little ones in your group, you'll probably want to pass on seeing them—or ride the Strip bus to get there.

The Arcade Awards

Hotels and restaurants are often ranked with stars, diamonds, and the like. We're not so precise in our rankings, but we can give you an idea of which arcades the young—and not so young—people who live in Las Vegas think are the best. Factors included in making this assessment include number and quality of games, attractiveness, general atmosphere, and the security factor.

Though it's one of the oldest, **Circus Circus** (702/734-

0410) is considered to have the best arcade games in the city. They're on the mezzanine, along with the ring in which the circus acts perform. A big part of the Circus Circus games' appeal comes from the colorful surroundings and the aura of excitement generated on the midway.

Gameworks at Showcase Mall (3785 Las Vegas Boulevard S.; 702/432-4263), which is new and enormous, ranks second on our list. The ultimate of the games is Vertical Reality. Once inside Vertical Reality, players race against the clock, taking their cues from a seventeen-foot-high screen that represents a three-story building where their foe, Mr. Bigg, lives in a penthouse. There are about 280 more games—most of them of the video and arcade kinds. Open from 10:00 A.M. to 4:00 A.M., other features include a climbing wall and my favorite, a photo concession that, among its other capabilities, can "morph" photos of humans and animals. A special promotion at Gameworks pairs lunch and an hour of timed game play.

Sega Virtualand Arcade at Luxor (702/262-4000), according to our experts, rates a third place. Among the most popular games in the 18,000-square-foot facility are the Virtual Formula Race Cars and F-16 Flight Simulators.

Among the arcades in other hotel/casinos and shopping centers, those at **Treasure Island, Caesars Palace, Bally's,** the **Riviera,** and **Excalibur** have the reputation of being the best. My choice among them is Treasure Island, since it's themed throughout and a uniformed security guard is prominently present.

According to responsible Las Vegas parents, no children under the age of twelve should be left alone at the arcades, and even teenagers should be cautioned about adults who behave inappropriately. As the result of an expansion of an existing curfew law, which went into effect in September 1997, children under eighteen years of age are barred from Las Vegas–area arcades between 10:00 P.M. and 5:00 A.M.

weekdays and from midnight to 5:00 A.M. on weekends. The law also requires that security guards be posted in arcades (rooms with a minimum of twenty coin-operated amusement machines) and that other security measures, such as surveillance cameras, be used to monitor areas with fewer machines. The new law also establishes guidelines for training guards on how to spot potential pedophiles and child stalkers.

The Fremont Experience

Glitter Gulch is another name for Las Vegas's downtown. And yes, the lights are brighter there. Always have been. Even before the **Fremont Experience** you could stand on the street corner and read a newspaper at midnight.

Now the lights are even more dazzling, for some 2.1 million of them, set in a ninety-foot-high Space Frame, illuminate a 1,400-foot-long stretch above a traffic-free mall along Fremont Street.

The Fremont Experience, which debuted in late 1995, is a light-and-sound extravaganza. Presented on the hour from 8:00 P.M. to midnight, the multisensory production makes use of thirty-one computers that synchronize the lights (65,536 color combinations are possible) with special effects and music.

Five different shows have been produced so far. Each of them lasts eight minutes, and they're alternated so that if you stay around for two or three shows, you won't see the same one twice. Exotic flowers unfold and planes streak in formation overhead in "Odyssey's" finale. Dancers do-si-do and coyotes howl in "Country Western Nights," and "Las Vegas Legends" features a potpourri of Las Vegas sights and sounds. The other shows are "Swing Cats" and "Heartbeat of the Planet."

Beneath the Space Frame, patterned walkways punctuated by palm trees, kiosks, and pushcarts have been transformed into one of the city's most pleasant places to stroll. Along the five-block pedestrian promenade, brightly painted vendors' carts brim with the kinds of merchandise that youngsters "just gotta have"—miniature cars, stuffed toys, key chains, and cool sunglasses. Jugglers, zebra-striped mimes, and musicians stroll along, while bands play on the mobile stages. Top professionals, such as the Doveiko Aerialists, stars of the Moscow Circus, also perform. The Fremont Experience is becoming an increasingly popular venue for the city's fairs and festivals, too.

There are other attractions downtown—the world's largest slot machine at the **Four Queens** (202 Fremont Street; 702/385-4011), and the **Las Vegas Club** (18 Fremont Street; 702/385-1164), advertised to have the largest collection of baseball memorabilia other than that at the Baseball Hall of Fame in Cooperstown, New York.

Added Attractions

Two hotel/casinos in outlying parts of the city also have free attractions that you might enjoy if you don't have to go very far out of your way to see them. At **Rio Suite Hotel/Casino** (3700 W. Flamingo Road; 702/247-7964), the Masquerade Show in the Sky, presented every two hours beginning at noon on Sunday, Tuesday, and Thursday, and at 1:00 P.M. on Friday and Saturday, features fantasy floats that glide on tracks thirteen feet above the casino floor. A cast of thirty-six lavishly costumed dancers, musicians, and bungee aerialists add to the spectacle. Sunset Stampede, at **Sam's Town Hotel and Gambling Hall** (5111 Boulder Highway; 702/456-7777), presents a laser light and water show at 2:00 P.M., 6:00 P.M., 8:00 P.M., and 10:00 P.M. The show is most effective after dark, when you can see the colors of the lights playing on the water.

Though the **Liberace Museum** (1775 E. Tropicana Avenue; 702/798-5595) isn't casino sponsored, it has a strong relationship with casino shows, since Liberace was one of the most glittering Las Vegas showroom performers and made the city his home. The museum, composed of three exhibit areas, chronicles "Mr.

Showmanship's" dazzling career. The Piano, Car, and Celebrity Galleries make up the main museum. The Costume and Jewelry Galleries as well as re-creations of Liberace's office and bedroom from his Palm Springs hacienda, the Cloisters, are located in the Annex. The Library displays the entertainer's miniature-piano collection—one of them is made from thousands of toothpicks— and a photo history of his life and family.

One customized auto in the Car Gallery is covered with rhine- stones. A Rolls-Royce's surface is composed of thousands of mir- ror tiles. More mirror tiles decorate Liberace's favorite Baldwin grand in the Piano Gallery, whereas jewels, feathers, satin, and fur add to the flamboyance of his onstage wardrobe displayed on mannequins and hangers in the Costume Gallery.

The collection is eclectic, to say the least, with several hun- dred pieces of rare Moser crystal from the former Czechoslo- vakia, a set of dinnerware formerly owned by John F. Kennedy, an inlaid crucifix presented to Liberace by Pope Pius XII, and the entertainer's candelabra ring with platinum candlesticks and diamond flames among the memorabilia on display. The museum is open Monday through Saturday, 10:00 A.M. to 5:00 P.M.; Sunday, 1:00 to 5:00 P.M. (bus 201).

The **Imperial Palace Auto Collection,** located on the fifth floor of the Imperial Palace Hotel/Casino's parking garage (3535 Las Vegas Boulevard S.; 702/731-3311), showcases cars of the rich, famous, and infamous. Among the important vehicles on display are the king of Siam's 1928 Delage, Pope Paul VI's 1966 Chrysler Imperial, Adolf Hitler's 1939 Mercedes-Benz, Juan Peron's 1939 straight-8 Packard, and Al Capone's 1930 V-16 Cadillac.

Showbiz wheels on display include W.C. Fields' 1938 Cadillac, Tom Mix's 1937 Cord, and motorcycles owned by Steve McQueen, Clark Gable, and Sammy Davis, Jr.

There are cars that made automotive history, too—a 1910 Thomas Flyer and the largest gathering of Model J. Duesenbergs in the world. Although the auto collection has grown to more than 750 antique, classic, and special-interest vehicles, only two hundred of them are on display at one time. The museum is open daily from 9:30 A.M. to 11:00 P.M. Although an admission is charged, it's not difficult to find coupons for free admission in the entertainment magazines.

Adults of a certain age won't want to miss **Elvis-A-Rama** (3401 Industrial Road; 702/309-7200). And fortunately, whether kids are Elvis fans or not, they'll most likely enjoy it, too. Featuring original Elvis Presley personal items and memorabilia (estimates range between $3 million and $5 million worth), the exhibits are well designed. Continually playing records of "The King" singing his best-known numbers adds to the total effect.

Among the displays in this 8,200-square-foot museum are the "Peacock" and "Cisco Kid" jumpsuits that Elvis wore in Las Vegas performances (from 1969 to 1977, he sold out 837 consecutive shows). There are guitars, his 1955 Cadillac limo, and his $75,000 ruby ring, as well as his army uniforms, record jackets, posters, and—of course—his blue suede shoes.

In 2001 various coupons in entertainment magazines could be redeemed for a free Elvis-a-Rama bear when one general admission ticket was purchased, a free T-shirt with general admission ticket purchase, and two tickets for the price of one.

Star Trek: The Experience (Las Vegas Hilton, 3000 Paradise Road; 702/697-TREK), as its name implies, is more than a ride or show. Its sound, motion, and detail transports participants to the twenty-fourth century. Aboard the Starship USS *Enterprise,* they can fire photon torpedoes and battle aliens, while space taxis and delivery ships whizzing by create the illusion of flying around the globe. The $70 million production includes "Voyage through Space," a twenty-two-minute simulated adventure; the "History of the Future Museum," the world's largest permanent collection of authentic Star Trek costumes, props and memorabilia; a restaurant; and a lounge. Dedicated Trekkies will wish to purchase an all-day pass.

Madame Tussaud's Celebrity Encounter (the Venetian; 3355 Las Vegas Boulevard S.; 702/367-1847), the first of

Madame Tussaud's wax museums in the United States, features five themed settings showcasing more than one hundred of the western world's most famous stars of film, TV, music, and sports. In the "Sports Arena," Muhammad Ali and Evander Holyfield pose in a boxing ring. Tennis star John McEnroe, baseball great Babe Ruth, and olympian Florence Griffith Joyner are among the other famous athletes re-created in wax.

"The Big Night" portrays a VIP party in an art deco setting, with actors Arnold Schwarzenegger and Whoopi Goldberg as well as TV host Oprah Winfrey among the guests. "Las Vegas Legends" include singers Judy Garland and Liza Minelli; comedians Bob Hope and George Burns; and entertainers Tony Bennett, Marilyn Monroe, and Frank Sinatra, with mobster Bugsy Siegel gazing on from a bench along the wall. Rounding out the exhibits are a series of graphic displays explaining the wax-figure producing process; the "Rock and Pop" room; and "The Finale," a multimedia theatrical tribute to the Las Vegas legends, featuring music, movie clips, and an Elvis impersonator.

The walk-through **Lion Habitat** (MGM Grand; 3799 Las Vegas Boulevard S.; 702/891-1111) is truly an amazing place. Featuring three levels with rock outcroppings, four waterfalls, a pond and living acacia trees, it re-creates the Savannah-like natural surroundings of the magnificent animals on display. The glass walls and viewing tunnel throughout the facility allow visitors to look at the lions from a variety of perspectives.

The eighteen lions, whose days on display are rotated, live in air conditioned quarters at trainer Keith Evan's spread when they aren't on exhibit. Three of the lions—Goldie, Metro, and Baby Lion—are direct descendants of the original MGM marquee lion.

Though it's fascinating any time, the attraction is at its best when there are lion cubs in the nursery. Separated from the main area, the nursery is where the baby lions are socialized by playing with their human caretakers.

The **Shark Reef** (Mandalay Bay; 3950 Las Vegas Boulevard

S.; 702/632-4555) contains 1.3 million gallons of sea water and 2,000 dangerous and/or unusual sea creatures, including a dozen varieties of sharks. More than seventy-five species of both tropical and freshwater fish are on display, too, as are crocodiles, vividly green colored tree pythons (with razor-sharp teeth), and all sorts of dangerous snakes in the Serpents & Dragons exhibit. Divers in scuba gear get into the tank at feeding time.

At the **Omnimax Theatre** (Caesars Palace, 3570 Las Vegas Boulevard S., 702/731-7900), viewers fly high above the Rocky Mountains, dive under the sea to get close-up views of the sharks, and do all sorts of amazing things, thanks to a huge dome-shaped screen plus a nine-channel "Sensaround" sound system of eighty-nine speakers. Shows are presented every hour from 2:00 P.M. to 10:00 P.M. (additional shows at 1:00 and 11:00 P.M. on Friday and Saturday).

There's also an **IMAX** theater at Luxor, where three movies alternate on a 68-by-84-foot screen. Spectators wear special lightweight visors in order to experience the sensation of being in the cockpit of an Indy car, diving underwater to frolic with playful sea lions, and speeding through the galaxies on a space station (702/262-4555).

Advertised as "the most hair-raising experience in Las Vegas," the **Cinema Ride in 3-D** (Forum Shops at Caesars; 702/369-4008) features four 3-dimensional adventures. "Atlantis" involves an underseas submarine chase. "Coaster Crazy" takes participants on a roller coaster ride, complete with jostles, scraping noises, and an eerily realistic plunging sensation. "Galactic Flight" and "Haunted Graveyard" feature additional thrills, chills, and bumps.

The **Magic and Movie Hall of Fame** at O'Shea's Casino (3555 Las Vegas Boulevard S.; 702/737-1343) displays what is advertised as a "multi-million-dollar exhibit of magic, movie, and ventriloquist memorabilia." Although it's open Wednesday through Sunday from 10:00 A.M. to 6:00 P.M., the best time to visit is in the afternoon, since mini-magic shows at 2:00, 3:00, and 4:00 P.M. are included in the admission price.

Non-Neon Attractions

Sometimes youngsters aren't as bedazzled by Las Vegas glitter as they are by traditional amuseuments such as those at **Scandia Family Fun Center** (paralleling the west side of I-15 at 2900 Sirius Avenue; 702/364-0700).

The mini-structures on the miniature golf course ($5.50 per player) are based upon Scandinavian buildings and include a medieval castle, a lighthouse, a church, and a windmill. There are bumper boats and raceway cars ($3.95), arcade games, and batting cages. For $14.95 you can buy an "Unlimited Wristband," good for all activities for one day. The "Super Saver," which includes one round of golf, two rides, and five arcade tokens, costs $10.95.

Another favorite with local children is **Mountasia Family Fun Center** (2050 Olympic Avenue; 702/898-7777) with bumper boats, go-karts, roller skating, and more than seventy-five video games. There's also a thirty-six-hole miniature golf course with desert surroundings, palm trees, and a lagoon. It's a pay-as-you-play amusement center, with go-karts and bumper cars and roller skating. Eighteen holes of miniature golf costs $4.00 for children under twelve, $5.50 for people over that age, or $14.00 for four people (a coupon for a free round of golf with the purchase of the same is readily available). There's also a Passport to Fun, which includes three go-kart rides and one bumper car ride, one roller-skating session, one round of golf, a small soft drink, and ten video game tokens. Mountasia is open Monday to Thursday from 3:00 P.M. to 10:00 P.M., Friday from 3:00 P.M. to midnight, Saturday from 10:00 A.M. to midnight, and Sunday from 10:00 A.M. to 10:00 P.M. (Locals with elementary and middle school–aged children prefer to have them play at Mountasia and other amusement centers during the early evening because of some of the older kids' behavior in the later hours.)

Las Vegas Gran Prix (1401 N. Rainbow Boulevard; 702/259-

7000) features go-karts, kiddy go-karts, and a video arcade. The emphasis, as its name implies, is on racing, with fast driving and tire squealing an important part of the action. All rides take one ticket. Kiddie Karts are for children four years old and up, and one ride lasts six minutes. The minimum height for go-karts is fifty-four inches, and these are five-minute rides. Drivers have to be sixteen years or older to drive the Gran Prix (three and a half times around the banked oval) and Super Stock Cars (two-minute timed ride).

Bonnie Springs and Old Nevada in Red Rock Canyon (702/875-4191) is a re-created Old West town with staged gun fights, stagecoach rides, shops, and a petting zoo among its attractions. The ranch, which was built in 1843 and served as a stopover for California-bound wagon trains, now features a re-created western frontier town, with historical exhibits and theatrical productions. If you've never been to a re-created amusement of this sort before, you might consider driving out. Bonnie Springs is open from 10:30 A.M. to 6:00 P.M. daily.

At the **Lied Discovery Children's Museum** (833 N. Las Vegas Boulevard; 702/382-5437), kids can crawl through Toddler Towers and tap a tune with their toes on the Musical Pathway. They can pilot the Space Shuttle, play disc jockey, and create color computer prints. In fact, this first-rate museum features more than one hundred hands-on exhibits and hosts many special programs throughout the year. Best of all, it lets adults play, too. Don't miss this one. Open Tuesday to Saturday from 10:00 A.M. to 5:00 P.M.; Sunday from 12:00 to 5:00 P.M. Across the street from the Lied, the **Las Vegas Museum of Natural History** (900 Las Vegas Boulevard N.; 702/384-3466) isn't as slick as its neighbor, but it is a worthwhile stop nonetheless. One reason is the animated dinosaurs, which make all sorts of horrific noises (though five- and six-year-olds adore them, smaller children can be terrified).

Small sharks swim in a three-hundred-gallon tank, and there's a hands-on children's room where kids can touch fossils, bones, and all sorts of other cool stuff. When you visit the museum, be sure to bring along one of its brochures for each child so that they each can receive a gift at the museum shop and science store. (The widely distributed brochures can be found in racks at car rental agencies, at tourist centers along the Strip, and at the Las Vegas Convention & Visitors Authority Visitor Center.) The museum is open daily from 9:00 A.M. to 4:00 P.M.

The **Clark County Heritage Museum** (1830 South Boulder Highway; 702/455-7955) brings history alive with an assortment of early-day buildings and machinery. On Heritage Street, five homes relocated from various parts of Nevada depict several periods of the state's history and are open to museum-goers. Each of the homes has been authentically restored to reflect the era in which it was built. Other displays on the museum grounds include a replicated newspaper print shop from the early 1900s, a re-created ghost town, and a collection of rolling stock, illustrating the Silver State's past. The museum is open daily from 9:00 A.M. to 4:30 P.M. except on major holidays.

The **Nevada State Museum and Historical Society** system is known throughout the country for the quality of its exhibits. At the Las Vegas branch of Nevada State Museum and Historical Society (Lorenzi Park; 700 Twin Lakes Drive; 702/486-5205), the Hall of Regional History focuses on the region's evolution from ancient Indian cultures through Spanish exploration, the railroad builders, and early settlers to modern times. The Hall of Biology explains Southern Nevada life zones, along with the plants and animal inhabitants (the stuffed animal displays are outstanding). The Changing Gallery exhibits encompass a wide range of subjects including historical, biological, and cultural aspects of the region. It's open 9:00 A.M. to 5:00 P.M. daily.

The **Marjorie Barrick Museum of Natural History** (4505 Maryland Parkway; 702/895-3381), located on the UNLV campus, focuses on southwestern desert reptiles, mammals, insects, archaeology, and anthropology. It's open from 9:00 A.M. to 5:00 P.M. Monday through Friday, and 10:00 A.M. to 5:00 P.M. on

Saturday, and admission is free. Bus 109 goes to the UNLV campus.

White tigers from the Himalayas, eagles, and 150 other species of animals and birds can be seen at the **Southern Nevada Zoological Park** (1775 N. Rancho Drive; 702/648-5955). Although residents include chimps, wallabies, parrots, and the only family of Barbary apes in the United States as well as every venomous reptile native to southern Nevada, the stars of the animal park as far as little kids are concerned may be the cows, chickens, pigs, and the warm and fuzzies they can hold in the petting zoo. The zoo is open daily from 9:00 A.M. to 5:00 P.M.

The **Planetarium at Community College** of Southern Nevada (3200 E. Cheyenne Avenue; 702/651-5059) explores the galaxy, the Great Barrier Reef, and other exciting parts of the universe in programs at 6:00 and 7:30 P.M. Friday, 3:30 and 7:30 P.M. Saturday.

Be a Star . . . or Maybe an Extra

Las Vegas glitter, the surrounding Old West countryside, and accessibility to Los Angeles make the area a natural shooting ground for films and TV productions. The **Nevada Motion Picture Division's Event Hotline** (702/486-2727) tells when and where movies and TV shows are currently being shot and what companies are in charge of casting. The city is also popular with foreign filmmakers, so you may see crews from cities such as Berlin, Singapore, or Tokyo.

Industrial Tours

The best industrial tour in town for your money—actually, the tour is free—is the **Ethel M Chocolate Factory/Cactus Garden** (2 Cactus Garden Drive, Henderson; 702/458-8864). At the factory, visitors file slowly past a long stretch of plate glass, looking at what is everyone's image of the perfect candy plant. Workers are dressed all in white, their hair covered with white baseball-style hats or hairnets. They make the candies with machines that mix the ingredients and coat them with chocolate in a large airy room with spotless white walls. Other workers stand at stainless steel tables, wrapping the chocolates in jewel-colored foil.

At the end of the tour, each participant is given a complimentary chocolate (you can, of course, buy boxes of them in the factory shop). Outside the plant is a delightful two-and-a-half-acre cactus garden. The plants, clearly identified, include some rare species that you aren't likely to see elsewhere.

Ron Lee's World of Clowns (330 Carousel Parkway, Henderson; 702/434-3920), primarily a store where all sorts of clowns are sold, offers a free thirty-five-minute self-guided tour. This is *not* the place to bring kids who can't keep their hands off the merchandise.

Ninety-minute guided tours of its Thunderbird planes are offered at **Nellis Air Force Base** north of the city on Tuesdays and Thursdays at 2:00 P.M. The tour lasts about an hour and includes a video presentation, a guided museum presentation, and the chance to look closely at a Thunderbird F-16. People wishing to attend the tour must be at the Nellis AFB Main Gate (at the intersection of Craig Road and Las Vegas Boulevard) by 1:30 P.M., where a gate guard will direct them to a parking location. From there they will board a bus that will take them to the Thunderbird hangar (phone 702/652-4018 for more information).

You can also take walk-in tours of **Old Las Vegas Mormon Fort** (908 Las Vegas Boulevard N.; 702/486-3511). The oldest historic site in Nevada is open from 8:00 A.M. to 3:30 P.M. As forts go, it's not very large or exciting, and parking is sometimes difficult, so this is an attraction that appeals primarily to people who have a special interest in either the westward movement or Mormon settlements.

The **Las Vegas-Clark County Library District** offers additional entertainment options. Two brochures—one listing dates and times of weekly story hours and the other listing special programs for children—are available at the main library or any of its branches, or by sending a stamped, self-addressed business-size envelope to the Las Vegas Library & District Headquarters, 833 Las Vegas Boulevard N., Las Vegas NV 89101 (702/382-3493).

Throughout the year, the Clark County Parks and Recreation Department, the City of Las Vegas Parks and Leisure Activities, and other organizations within the area sponsor recreational activities for people of all ages. Most of these activities, however, are part of programs of several weeks' duration.

How to Keep Cool in Las Vegas

There are times when the Las Vegas temperatures soar, but that doesn't mean tempers have to. To keep your cool, the following are highly recommended.

- Spend the afternoon at the Dolphin Habitat and the Secret Garden of Siegfried & Roy at the Mirage. Arrive at the habitat when it opens at 11:00 A.M., before the midday heat becomes oppressive. Watch the dolphins for a while, then find a bench in the garden. If you've brought your water bottles (they're a necessity on summer days in Las Vegas) and favorite books along, you can combine looking at the elephant, rare white lions, tawny Bengal tigers, panthers, and snow leopard with some quiet time. It costs $10 to visit both the Dolphin Habitat and the Secret Garden (children under the age of ten get in free). Don't plan this excursion for a Wednesday, however, because the Secret Garden is closed.

- Time your arrival at Sam's Town to coincide with the 2:00 P.M. presentation of Sunset Stampede. During the daytime, the show isn't much to look at—all you see are splashing geyser-type plumes of water—but it's incredibly refreshing to feel the spray.

- Put on your bathing suits, pack your favorite games, water bottles, and towels in backpacks, and head for Wet 'n Wild (2601 Las Vegas Boulevard S.; 702/734-0088). Whenever you begin to heat up, pop into the water and play games under the canvas shade areas in between times. There's information on the water park's features in the next chapter.

- Drive out State Highway 159 to Mt. Charleston (see chapter 10), where the temperatures are at least ten (and can be thirty) degrees cooler than in Las Vegas.

- Stop by Hawaiian Shave Ice at 4001 S. Decatur Boulevard (702/365-9685) for shaved ice in a variety of flavors or at any of the Wendy's drive-throughs for their large-size Frosties. For about a dollar apiece, you'll cool down in a hurry.

- If you or your children water ski, rent a boat and skis at one of the marinas on Lake Mead. Be sure, however, that you follow water safety rules.

- Go to Floyd Lamb State Park, known to the locals as Tule Springs. Just ten miles north of Lake Vegas on Tule Springs Road, it was an early watering spot for the Indians. Within the park are fishing lakes, swimming and picnic facilities, birds—some exotics, others in their natural habitats—and shade trees.

Wherever you go, don't forget the sunscreen.

Houses of Worship

Families to whom worship is an important part of their lives will find that there are more churches, synagogues, and other places of worship in Las Vegas per capita than in any other city in the United States. A listing that follows includes only a sampling of the more than five hundred:

Spring Valley Baptist Church
3135 S. Rainbow Boulevard
702/871-0150

Guardian Angel Cathedral (Roman Catholic)
302 E. Desert Inn Road
702/735-5241

Located just off the Strip, Guardian Angel has both Sunday and Saturday afternoon masses.

Christ Church (Episcopal)
2000 S. Maryland Parkway
702/735-7655

Temple Beth Sholom (Conservative united)
10700 Havenwood Lane
702/804-1333

Congregation Shaarei Tefilla (Orthodox)
Forman-Glick
1331 S. Maryland Parkway
702/384-3565

Adat Ari El (Reformed)
3310 S. Jones Boulevard
702/221-1230

Mountain View Lutheran Church (Missouri synod)
9550 W. Cheyenne Avenue
702/360-8290

University United Methodist Church
4412 S. Maryland Parkway
702/733-7157

Las Vegas Mormon Temple
827 Temple View Drive
702/435-0025

Annual Events

In addition to the year-round attractions, Las Vegas offers a host of special days throughout the year. Events such as Halloween haunted houses, and free jazz, bluegrass, and country music concerts downtown are put on by the **Clark County Parks and Recreation Department** (702/455-5417). The **Allied Art Council** (702/731-5417) and **Clark County Library** (702/733-7810) also sponsor entertainment that's fun for the whole family.

Some events, such as the free **Clark County Children's Festival,** held at the **Winchester Community Center** (3130 S. McLeod Drive; 702/455-8239) on a Saturday in the latter part of April, are specifically family oriented. The festival features crafts, contests, musical entertainment, and a dramatic performance.

One of the most delightful family-oriented events is the annual **Festival of Trees and Lights** at Opportunity Village (6300 W. Oakey Boulevard; 702/259-3700). Held in December, it features fifty decorated trees, a gingerbread village, professional entertainment, and music by local choirs. Children get to decorate their own gingerbread cookies, shop at a "kids only" gift shop, and make holiday crafts, too. Admission is nominal.

On three days during the **National Finals Rodeo** in December (see chapter 7) the **National Finals BBQ Cook-Off**

and Party is held at the Tropicana (702/739-2411). The event features thirty-six hours of live music performed by top country stars, free samples of barbecue concocted by one hundred professional teams of chefs, an exhibits pavilion, and BBQ village. Admission is $10 for adults and $5 for children under twelve.

One of the funniest annual events is the **Strut Your Mutt** in November at Dog Fancier's Park (5800 E. Flamingo Road; 702/455-7506), when canines of all shapes, sizes, and breeds are entered in a wacky competition.

Other annual events include the **Craft Fair and Rib Burn-Off** in May at Sunset Park (702/455-7506), which features handmade arts and crafts, live music, kids' activities, and food.

Almost any day of the year, some sort of special event is going on, and many of them—boat shows, national dance competitions, dollhouse and model train exhibits—may be of interest to your family. For more information, pick up one of Las Vegas's free entertainment magazines or newspapers, or contact the convention and visitor's authority.

The Las Vegas Halloween Scene

When any special day rolls around in Las Vegas, there are bound to be a number of special events put on to honor it. Take Halloween, for example. Most of the events are presented annually, but if one isn't, there are usually one or two others to take its place. In the past, Halloween events have included "Texas Screamer" haunted house, a thirteen-scene production at the Texas Station Gambling Hall & Hotel (2101 Texas Star Lane; 702/631-1000), which featured a mad doctor's laboratory, an execution chamber, and a surprise visit from the Texas chainsaw lunatic. The ghoulish extravaganza involved a dozen live actors and a variety of animatronic creations. A portion of the ticket proceeds from this event go to an elementary school in north Las Vegas.

A group of professional magicians are the creative force behind the "Screamers" haunted house located next to the Planet Mirth Magic Shop at 5115 S. Industrial Road, Suite 106 (702/798-0039). Proceeds from tickets to "Screamers," which is inhabited by ghosts, goblins, witches, and bloodsucking vampires, benefit such charities as the Animal Foundation of Nevada.

Other haunted houses include the Freakling Brothers Dungeon in the Montgomery Ward Plaza at the corner of Sahara and Decatur and the Freakling Brothers Black Box at the K-Mart Shopping Center at the corner of Bonanza Road and Nellis Boulevard. Several Halloween costume balls for adults are also held annually during the latter part of October at various hotel/casinos. Since the costumes tend toward the lavish, exotic, or downright bizarre, it's great fun to watch the partygoers arrive. To find out when and where the balls are being held, consult the events calendars of the free entertainment magazines.

Family Fun with Funbooks

Most casinos offer giveaways of some sort, often in the form of funbooks. These are booklets that contain coupons primarily aimed at gamblers with two-for-one bets, free nickels, and the like. These booklets often contain a few nongaming coupons, too. Some of them are for free gifts; others are "two for the price of one" food offers or of the "buy this and you'll get that free" variety.

If your family is running low on cash or simply gets a kick out of receiving something for nothing, you can have some extra entertainment cashing in casino coupons. The following works best if there's at least one adult for each child, since only adults can redeem the coupons.

Go through the coupons you've collected (see chapter 1) and decide which of the offers are worth the effort. Then organize the coupons so that those from casinos in the same area are in a logical order for collecting your freebies.

For example, Circus Circus usually has free gifts that kids will like, such as fanny-packs, hats, and such. Two smaller casinos, Slots-A-Fun and Silver City—both under the same ownership as Circus Circus and in the same area—also have coupons for free popcorn and other treats. There are usually people outside these casinos distributing coupons that are good for redemption in a sister casino; for instance, Silver City coupons are distributed outside Slots-A-Fun, and some of the coupons you receive at Silver City are good for redemption at Circus Circus.

Great edible freebies you might want to collect while you're in the Circus Circus area are the foot-long hot dogs, which used to be free with coupons from the Westward Ho, but now cost $.99 (2900 Las Vegas Boulevard S.; 702/731-2900). Be sure to grab a supply of paper napkins and a plastic knife from the serving counter so that you can cut these huge hot dogs into manageable portions.

The Tropicana funbooks include coupons for free admission to the hotel's gambling museum as well as food and beverage specials and discounts on show tickets, retail, and specialty shop purchases. At the Flamingo Hilton, one of the funbook coupons allows the holder to get a second burger and fries free when one burger and fries are purchased at the regular price.

Downtown, you can get free foot-longs—probably the best in town at any price—at Lady Luck Casino & Hotel (coupons for the free funbooks are found in both airline in-flight magazines and Las Vegas brochure racks). Other easy-to-find coupons are those for Fitzgeralds Holiday Inn (301 Fremont Street; 702/388-2400), where free gifts are kid-pleasers, such as mugs and digital watches that look like they're made from car tires.

Ethnic Celebrations

At last count, thirty-six ethnic organizations—ranging from the Sri Lanka Nevada Association and Sons of Norway to the Las Vegas Basque Club and the Cambodian Federation—were listed in the Las Vegas telephone directory. There's a Japanese-American club and an Egyptian-American Society, the Chilean-American Social Club, and the African-American Cultural Arts Foundation. And since these groups don't want to lose sight of their cultural traditions, most all of them hold annual celebrations, the majority of which are open to the public.

The largest ethnic group is Hispanic and comprises more than 11 percent of the city's population. Although the majority of them are of Mexican descent, large numbers of local Latinos came to the United States from Cuba or Central and South America. Due to the preponderance of Mexican-Americans, however, most of the annual celebrations have their origins in Mexico.

Cinco de Mayo, the annual festival celebrating the 1862 victory of the Mexican army over the French in Pueblo, Mexico, takes place at Freedom Park (corner of Mojave and E. Washington Avenue). It's a kaleidoscope of dancing, mariachis, piñatas, carnival games, fireworks, Mexican food, and crafts. You'll be surrounded with more of the same at the annual salute to **Mexican Independence Day** in September.

More than twenty Pacific Rim cultures are also represented by sizable populations. In September, the **Pacific Islands Festival** at Lorenzi Park (333 W. Washington Avenue) offers continuous music and dance entertainment, boutiques, arts and crafts, exhibits, and food booths. Other Asian celebrations include **Asian-Pacific Heritage Month** in May (Chinatown Plaza; 702/221-8448) and **Philippine Independence Day** in June (Charleston Heights Cultural Center, 800 S. Bush; 702/251-9330).

At the **Japan Festival** in November, there's a Friendship parade down Las Vegas Boulevard, traditional performing arts presentations in MGM Grand's Hollywood Theatre, and exhibitions, demonstrations, and workshops focusing on traditional Japanese culture in various other venues. The focal point of the **Chinese New Year** celebration with its traditional firecrackers and dragon is Chinatown Plaza. Dates vary from year to year between January 21 and February 19.

A public celebration of the African-American cultural holiday of **Kwanzaa** is held at the West Las Vegas Library and Theatre (951 W. Lake Mead Boulevard; 702/647-2117) in the latter part of December and early January. Dances, storytelling, crafts, and ethnic foods are all part of the festivities. There are also various activities held in conjunction with **Black History Month** and the **Cowboys of Color Invitational Rodeo** during February. More than 9 percent of Las Vegas residents are African-American.

Hanukkah and other Jewish holidays are celebrated with special services at Temple Beth Shalom (1600 E. Oakey Boulevard; 702/258-8961) and Congregation Ner Tamid (2761 Emerson Avenue; 702/733-6292).

The **Snow Mountain Pow Wow** at the Las Vegas Paiute Indian Reservation in May (702/386-0758), the **Clark County Basque Festival** (702/258-8961), the **Greek Food Festival** in September (702/221-8245), and the **Columbus Day Parade** (702/736-4293) in October are some of the other ethnic festivals held throughout the year).

At the Movies

Families who like to go to movie theaters will find they have choices galore, from first-runs—and an occasional world premiere—to foreign films and weekend *Rocky Horror Picture Show* screenings.

Many of Las Vegas movie theaters are multiple-screen facilities. Tickets to first-run features usually cost from $5 to $7 for

11

hildren under the age of twelve. Tickets at second-
st from $2.00 to $2.50 for people of all ages. Las
gas s only drive-in (Vegas 6 Drive-In Theatre; 4150 W. Carey
Avenue; 702/646-3565) costs $4.50 for each person in the car
who is over the age of twelve. There's no charge for passengers
under twelve years of age. Since showtimes vary, it's important to
phone the theater of your choice in advance.

Among the first-run theaters are:

Century Cinedome 12
851 S. Boulder Highway, Henderson
702/457-3700

Century Orleans 12
4500 W. Tropicana Avenue
702/277-3456

Century Rancho-Santa Fe Theater
5101 N. Rancho Drive
702/645-5518

Tickets are $4 for adults before 5:45 P.M., Monday to Friday
and before 2:00 P.M. on weekends.

Cinedome Theatres of Las Vegas
3200 S. Decatur Boulevard
702/362-2133

Red Rock Theatres
5201 W. Charleston Boulevard
702/870-1423

Bargains here are also the $4 tickets for matinees (before 6:00
P.M. on Monday to Friday and before 2:00 P.M. on weekends and
holidays).

Sunset Station Cinema
Sunset Station Casino
1301 W. Sunset Road, Henderson
702/221-2283

Texas 12 Theatres
Texas Station Casino
2101 Texas Star Lane
702/221-2283

Admission to shows before 6:00 P.M. is $3.75 rather than the regular $7.00 for adults.

United Artists Showcase Theatre
3769 Las Vegas Boulevard S.
702/740-4511

Second-run theaters include:

Cinema 8
3025 E. Desert Inn Road
702/734-2124

When you're deciding which movies to attend, you might see if any of the following—filmed wholly or in part in Nevada—are playing: *City Slickers, Father's Day, Honey, I Blew Up the Kids, Leaving Las Vegas, Rainman, Sister Act,* and *Sister Act II.*

CHAPTER 7

Activities

Las Vegas won't disappoint families who like physical activity; whose vacation happiness depends on facilities beyond hotel fitness rooms and swimming pools. Due to the number of people who visit the city and the days the sun shines, Las Vegas offers more recreational opportunities than most cities two or three times its size.

The Sporting Life

As far as golf courses, tennis courts, and racquet ball courts are concerned, many of them are open to the public and, in fact, depend on tourist business. The number and quality of the city's golf courses are especially impressive. The following list includes a sampling of the public courses and their fees.

Course	Holes/Par	Green Fees
Angel Park Golf Club 100 S. Rampart Blvd. 702/254-4653	18 (two) 71/72, 70; 12/3	$135, Mon.–Thurs. $155, weekends $80, twilight Clark County residents

Course	Holes/Par	Green Fees
		$85, $90, $45 (cart included) Club rental $40–$50
The Badlands at Peccole Ranch Resort 9119 Alta Dr. 702/242-4653	18/72	$135, Mon.–Thurs. $190, Fri.–Sun. $80–$90, twilight (includes cart and practice balls)
Black Mountain 500 Greenway Rd. 702/565-7933	18/72	$82, weekdays Henderson–$100 weekends (carts mandatory)
Boulder City Golf Course 1 Clubhouse Dr. Boulder City 702/293-9236	18/72	$45; $37, Clark County residents
Craig Ranch Golf 628 W. Craig Rd. 702/642-9700	18/70	$27 (includes cart) daily; $19, without cart
Desert Pines Golf Club 3415 E. Bonanza Rd. 702/366-1616	18/71	$115, Mon.–Thurs. $140, Fri.–Sun.
Desert Rose Golf Course 5483 Club House Dr. 702/431-4653	18/71	$69, Mon.–Thurs. $89, Fri.–Sun. residents, $33, $39
Desert Willow Golf Club 2020 W. Horizon Ridge Pkwy. Henderson 702/263-4653	18/70	$45 (walk) $55 (cart)

Course	Holes/Par	Green Fees
Las Vegas Golf Club 4300 W. Washington Ave. 702/646-3003	18/72	$69, weekdays $89, weekends residents, $24.50–$33.75
Las Vegas Paiute Resort 10325 Nu-Way Kaiv Blvd. (Snow Mountain exit) 702/658-1400	18 (two)/72	$145, Mon.–Thurs. $160, Fri.–Sun.
Legacy Golf Club 130 Par Excellence Dr. Henderson 702/897-2187	18 (two)/72	$115, Mon.–Thurs. $125, Fri.–Sat. June to Sept. 8, $55, $65
Los Prados Golf Country Club 5150 Los Prados Circle 702/645-5696	18/70	$35, Mon.–Thurs. $45, weekends
North Las Vegas Golf Club 324 E. Brooks Ave. 702/633-1833	9/27	$6.00 to $8.50, depending on day/time; student, senior rates available
Painted Desert Golf Course 5555 Painted Mirage Dr. 702/645-2570	18/72	$100–$130, Mon.-Thurs. $130–$160, Fri.–Sun.; twilight rates
Reflection Bay Hyatt Regency Lake Las Vegas 75 Montelago Blvd. Henderson 702/740-4653	18/72	$250, spring, fall $190, summer (discount for Hyatt Regency guests)

Course	Holes/Par	Green Fees
The Revere at Anthem 2600 Evergreen Oaks Dr. 702/259-4653	18/72	$125–$150, Mon.–Thurs. $155–$180, Fri.-Sun.
Rio Secco Golf & Country Club 2851 Grand Hills Dr. Henderson 702/889-2444	18/72	$200, Harrah's & Rio Suite guests; $250, others
(Tiger Woods works out with his teacher, Butch Harmon, here.)		

As you can see, green fees vary a lot (most green fees include cart; club rentals range from $5 to $50). At most courses in Las Vegas—and there are more than three dozen—green fees for summertime play are significantly lower than during the cooler months.

What you can't tell from prices alone is what the courses are like. Angel Park's "Cloud Nine," for example, is unique in that it re-creates twelve of the most famous par-3 holes in the world, including the double green at St. Andrews and the Postage Stamp at Royal Troon.

The Badlands course is built around arroyos. The $12 million Desert Pines course features some three thousand pine trees measuring from ten to forty feet tall. The Las Vegas Hilton Country Club was the site of Tiger Wood's first pro win at the Las Vegas Invitational. Pete Dye designed the course at Las Vegas Paiute Resort; Billy Casper and Greg Nash were the architects for Sun Valley Las Vegas Golf Club courses.

In addition to the courses, two practice facilities, **Green Valley Golf Range** (1351 Warm Springs Road; 702/434-4300) and **Las Vegas International Golf Center** (4813 Paradise Road; 702/650-9002), are open twenty-four hours, with multiple night-lighted tees and putting greens.

When you're flexible as to tee times and which courses you want to play, **Stand-by Golf** (702/597-2665) can save you up to

25 percent on same-day or next-day reservations. By 5:00 P.M. each day, Stand-by has information from the courses it contracts with as to which tee times are available at discounted prices. Phone after 7:00 A.M. for same-day play and from 5:00 P.M. to 9:00 P.M. for the following day.

Tennis Anyone?

If tennis is your game, you'll be able to play it on dozens of courts located throughout the city. The courts maintained by the county and city parks and recreation departments are almost always less expensive than privately run tennis operations, but are less convenient for most tourists. The following list includes those courts, both public and private, that will be easiest for the majority of tourists to get to.

Facility	Number of Courts	Fees
Flamingo Hilton Tennis Club 702/696-9705	4 lighted, hitting alley	$20, Las Vegas residents; guests at Bally's, Paris, and Flamingo, $12
Jackie Gaughan's Plaza Hotel 702/386-2110	4 lighted	hotel guests only (no racket rental) complimentary
Las Vegas Hilton Hotel 702/732-5111	6, 4 lighted	hotel guests only racket rental $10
Monte Carlo Las Vegas Blvd. S. 702/730-7777	4 lighted	$12 per court for one hour, guests; $18, nonguests
Paradise Park 4770 S. Harrison 702/455-7513	2 lighted	free; first come, first served

Facility	Number of Courts	Fees
Riviera Hotel 702/734-5110, ext. 9679	2 lighted	hotel guests free $10, nonguests per hour
The Sporting House 3025 Industrial Rd. 702/733-8999	2	$15 daily pass can also be used for racquetball
Sunset Park Tennis Sunset and Eastern Aves.	8 lighted	$3 per hour, day $5 per hour, night
YMCA 4141 Meadows Lane 702/877-9622	5 lighted	$10 day pass plus $3 allows unlimited play

Racquetball and Bowling

Raquetball players and bowlers will also have venues at which to pursue their sports. Among the most conveniently located raquetball courts are:

Facility	Number of Racquetball Courts	Fees
Las Vegas Athletic Club 1071 E. Sahara Ave. 702/734-5822	5	$15, day pass ($10 for hotel guest with room key or other proof)
The Sporting House 3025 Industrial Rd. 702/733-8999	12	daily pass $15

The larger bowling facilities—several of which host national tournaments—are:

Facility	Number of Bowling Lanes	Fees
Gold Coast 4000 W. Flamingo 702/367-7111	70	per game $2.25 shoes $1.75
Sam's Town Bowling Center 5111 Boulder Highway 702/454-8022	56	per game $1.25– $2.25; discounted prices, seniors, juniors shoes $1.50
Santa Fe 4949 Rancho Dr. N. 702/658-4995	60	$1.75–$2.40 shoes $2
Sunset Lanes 4565 E. Sunset Green Valley 702/736-2695	40	$1.25–$2.50; hourly, children, senior rates available shoes $2
Orleans Hotel & Casino 4500 W. Tropicana Ave. 702/365-7400	70	$1.75–$2.40
Castaways (formerly Showboat) 2800 Fremont St. 702/385-9153	106	$1.25–$2.25
Terrible's Town Casino & Bowl 642 S. Boulder Highway 702/564-7118	16	$1.00–$1.50 shoes $1.00–$1.25

All bowling alleys have varying rates, based upon customer's age, bowling status (league or open bowler), day of week and time of day, such as the graveyard shift at Orleans and Castaways.

Skating, Swimming, and Such

The **Ice Gardens** (3896 Swenson Street; 702/731-1062) features two rinks—one for ice hockey and the other for figure skating. Learn-to-skate programs, daily memberships, and skate rentals are available. Surya Bonaly, five-time European women's ice skating champion, practices there when she is at her home in Las Vegas. The only ice skating rink in a Las Vegas casino is at the **Santa Fe Hotel** (702/658-4991). Sessions last two hours, except on Saturday and Sunday afternoons when they're three hours. The hours of the sessions vary.

The **Crystal Palace Skating Centers** (3901 N. Rancho Drive; 702/645-4892; and 9295 W. Flamingo Road; 702/253-9832) offers roller skating each evening of the week, with afternoon sessions added on Saturday and Sunday. Tuesday is family night, when families of four or less can skate for a total of $10, including skate rental.

If the adults in your party want to attend a show, go out to dinner, or gamble, you might drop the youngsters off at the new Kids Quest operations at Sunset Station (702/547-7777) and Boulder Station (702/432-7777) and other casinos in the Station chain, where they can have fun with the Playano (playing tunes by walking on its giant keys), work on putting together the puzzle wall, operate a scale model excavator, project images on the shadow wall, sing along with favorite songs, watch themselves on a large TV screen, or get involved in lots of other exciting activities. Computer stations are located at each of the facilities, which are the most elaborate of Las Vegas casino child care centers. Kids Quest accepts children between six weeks and twelve years old; prices are $5 per child per hour, Monday through Thursday;

$6 on Friday, Saturday, and Sunday. Snacks cost $.75 each and drinks, $.50.

The Gold Coast has free child care for up to three and a half hours from 9:00 A.M. to midnight. The service is available for youngsters two to eight years old. Kids Tyme at the Orleans and Suncoast casinos costs $5 an hour for children from six months to twelve years. Video games, crafts, and a two-level "tunnel" play area keep the kids busy.

MGM Grand Youth Center was created specifically for children from three to twelve years old. Arts and crafts, activities, games, plus movies make this a popular place. The service is available to MGM Grand guests, but also on a limited basis to guests at other hotels. Parents must remain in the hotel/casino where the child care facility is located. There are extra charges for snacks and/or meals when they are available.

When the weather's chilly, it's still possible to go swimming, even though Las Vegas hotel/casinos don't have indoor pools. At the **Lorin L. Williams Municipal Indoor Pool** (Basic High School, 500 N. Palo Verde Drive, Henderson; 702/565-2123) there's indoor swimming on Tuesday, Thursday, Saturday, and Sunday. Swimmers can also enjoy the **YMCA** (4141 Meadows Lane; 702/877-9622). Admission is $10 for adults, $5 for teenagers thirteen to seventeen, and $4 for children twelve and under. The $15 family ticket admits two adults and however many children constitute the family group. Several sports clubs in the Las Vegas/Henderson orbit are also open to the public, but charge $10 to $15 a day, as opposed to less than $2 for the public facilities.

Total Immersion

The zenith of a Las Vegas vacation for kids who love the water could be a day at **Wet 'n Wild** (2601 Las Vegas Boulevard S.; 702/734-0088), a twenty-six-acre park packed with water-related activities. There's the half-million-gallon Surf Lagoon with ocean-size waves and a thrill wall called Banzai-Banzai. The Bomb Bay drops people feet first from a big capsule into the water.

Willy-Willy, named for an Australian whirlwind, spins riders in a hydra-hurricane on a clockwise course around a ninety-foot-diameter pool at a speed of 10 miles per hour.

The Black Hole is not for people who are claustrophobic, but the enclosed flume ride is one of the attractions that feature two-person tubes, so a kid (or parent) who's scared doesn't have to go it alone.

Der Stuka is said to be the fastest water chute in the world. At a seventy-degree angle, riders more or less freefall seventy-six feet to a straight one hundred-foot runway that slows them down before arriving at the catch pool.

Though younger children find the water park concept exciting, many of them are scared—and some actually petrified—of going down the big slides. They'll probably prefer floating around on the Lazy River and spending their time in the Children's Water Playground, with its mini-size water slides, water cannons, and bouncing Lily Pads. The centerpiece of the playground is the Fujifilm Blimp, complete with squirt guns and other exciting features.

In addition to the water rides and attractions, the park includes volleyball courts, horseshoe pits, tetherballs, and sandboxes, as well as picnic tables and shaded areas. Brochure maps of the various attractions' locations are available at the main entrance, as well as sheets that list the ratings of the attractions—low-speed, moderate, aggressive (requiring rider control and/or strong swimming skills), and high speed (can be stressful to those who fear heights, high speed, or enclosed places). It's a good idea for parents who plan to leave their children at the park to have an understanding with them regarding the rides they are allowed to go on. All nonswimmers must be accompanied by an adult who can swim. If you do leave the children, don't leave them without their water bottles and plenty of sunscreen.

During the summer, Wet 'n Wild averages between three thousand and five thousand visitors a day, but on at least one occasion, that number reached ten thousand. The park is big enough, however, and on average days the lines aren't excessively long.

Wet 'n Wild operates from early May until late September. The park opens each day at 10:00 A.M., but closing hours vary. From late June to early August it's open until 11:00 P.M., with live music, contests (prizes include airfares to Los Angeles, trips to Hawaii, T-shirts, sunglasses, and gift certificates), and games in addition to the water attractions.

All-day admission for people ten years and older is $25.95. It's $19.95 for children under 48 inches. Children under the age of three years get in free. Discount coupons for $2 off daily admission and value packs admitting four at approximately 25 percent off regular price are available in the free entertainment magazines and at tourist center brochure racks. Other promotions pair visits to Wet 'n Wild with other attractions as well as with meal deals.

Other Games People Play

Whether or not you're an expert, you might want to try out the eighteen-hole frisbee golf course at **Sunset Park** (Sunset and Eastern Avenues). Several other special interest facilities, also maintained by Clark County, are open to the public. They include the **Circus Circus Remote Control Car Track** for 1/4-, 1/8-, and 1/10-scale cars, at 6800 E. Russell Road and the **Clark County Archery Range** on the same site, recognized as one of the finest facilites of its type. The **Nellis Meadows Bicycle Motocross Track** (BMX), at 4949 East Cheyenne, is operated by Clark County Parks and Recreation in conjunction with the

National BMX League. Each rider is required to join the National Bicycle League, and all minors must have a parent's written permission to take part in any race (702/457-4617 or 702/876-9100).

The country around Las Vegas—except during the hot days of summer—is great for horseback and mountain bike riding. From flat desert paths to the cool arroyos of Red Rock Canyon, terrain goes from easy to moderately difficult to challenging. Most of the horseback adventures offered are of the guided-trail-ride variety. **Red Rock Canyon Riding Stables** (1211 S. Eastern Street; 702/387-2457) offers half-day, full-day, and overnight Cowboy Trail Rides to such places as Mt. Charleston, Brown Stone, and Valley of Fire. Most of the rides last four hours, but there are two-hour beginner's rides as well. Most popular is the sunset ride that offers views of Las Vegas as the lights begin glimmering in the dusk. After the ride, a barbecue dinner is served around the campfire. Prices vary with length of ride and amenities (see chapter 10).

If you prefer riding bicycles, a number of options—escorted or on your own—are available. Most of the desert rides are easy, since the valley floor is primarily flat. Cyclists in search of some moderate technical challenges may choose the eight-mile Cottonwood Valley Mountain Bike Park-Loop, which begins in the town of Blue Diamond off State Highway 160. The eight-and-one-half-mile Black Canyon Vista round-trip to Lake Mead National Recreation Area is moderately difficult.

The Red Rock–Wilson Cliffs Loop offers spectacular views of the Sandstone Bluffs and the Red Rock Recreation Lands. The forty-one-mile ride takes from five to nine hours to complete and is suitable for families with lots of stamina and biking experience.

The Bristlecone Pine trail in the Spring Mountains National Recreation Area and the River Mountain Peak trail separating Las Vegas and Henderson are two additional options in the moderate-to-difficult range (see chapter 10 for more information).

And for the Really Adventurous

The very thought of bungee-jumping gives me the willies, but I am sure there are families—or at least members thereof—who think it's the greatest, so here's the scoop. You go to **A.J. Hackett Bungy** at 810 Circus Circus Drive (702/385-4321), rise to the top of the 175-foot tower via an air conditioned "bungee elevator," pay your $54 ($25 for subsequent jumps, every fourth jump free), take a look at the Strip below, and jjjjjjjjjjuuuuuuuuuummmmmmmmmmp! You get a free membership card and certificate with your first jump. Other possibilities at A.J. Hackett include a 90,000-gallon dipping pool, day and night jumps, and bungee weddings.

If bungee jumping is too tame, you might try indoor skydiving. **Flyaway** (200 Convention Center Drive; 702/731-4768) consists of a twenty-minute training class, a fifteen-minute equipment preparation session, and a three-minute flight. Minors must be accompanied by parents in order to participate.

Spectator Sports

When you tire—literally and figuratively—of participating, you can still be involved in sports as a spectator. Las Vegas offers what well may be the most extensive and diverse array of professional sporting events in the world. It doesn't have major league baseball (plans to build spring training facilities were scrapped in 1997 after a three-year effort), but it has just about everything else. With events including professional world title boxing matches, hydroplane racing on Lake Mead, international table tennis championships, the National Finals Rodeo, and celebrity and professional golf tournaments, Las Vegas is where a good deal of the country's sports action is.

Some of the events are free or low-cost, like the annual Las Vegas Invitational Slo-Pitch Senior Softball Tournament, which takes place in August at various fields around the city; or the Las Vegas Holiday Prep Classic, in which high school basketball teams compete at UNLV North and South Gyms just before Christmas.

Others, like championship boxing matches—held at Caesars Palace, MGM Grand, and Mirage—are definitely for the big spenders. But although ringside seats can cost hundreds of dollars—more if you buy the tickets from the scalpers—you can see the boxers work out with their sparring partners prior to the big event for free. The more important the match, the earlier the boxers come into town. That means that workouts open to the public are usually the weekend before the fight for the biggest-name boxers, and on the first part of the week before the fight for lesser-knowns.

The Las Vegas 51s, a Triple A affiliate of the Los Angeles Dodgers in the Pacific Coast League, play their home games at **Cashman Field** (850 Las Vegas Boulevard N.; 702/386-7184; bus 113 or 208), and it's usually pretty good baseball. In fact, dozens of Las Vegas farm team players have made it to the majors in less than twenty years. For information on whom the 51s are playing and when, call their Hot Line at 702/739-3900.

Throughout the year, prestigious golf tournaments and tennis matches also take place at various Las Vegas venues. The best way to find out what sporting events are going on while your family is in town is by reading the free weekly/monthly entertainment magazines and the *Las Vegas Review Journal*.

The **National Finals Rodeo** (702/260-8605), the premier event of the Professional Rodeo Cowboys of America (PRCA), is held in Las Vegas each December. During the ten-day event, the country's top bull, bareback, and bronc riders, calf and steer ropers, and barrel racers compete for prize money. It's the time when the regular country music productions are augmented by even more country performances throughout the city, and the National Finals BBQ Cook-Off and Party is held.

Auto racing fans will want to check out the 480-acre **Las**

Vegas Motor Speedway (7000 N. Las Vegas Boulevard; 702/644-4443). The speedway features paved and dirt short tracks, a 4,000-foot-long drag strip, and a number of road courses and facilities for various kinds of vehicles—including go-karts. Spectator events run the gamut from the AMA Superbike Series season finale to NASCAR truck and racecar competitions. Prices vary with the events.

CHAPTER 8

After Dark Entertainment

L as Vegas is a town where even the strictest parents become flexible about bedtime. For nighttime entertainment is one of the city's major attractions. Nighttime options include not only entertainment that's a part of the casino scene, but performances sponsored by a variety of groups and organizations throughout the community. And some of it is just too good to miss.

Twenty years ago, Las Vegas casino entertainment centered around big-name stars—people like Frank Sinatra and Liza Minelli, who entertained in its showrooms. Then came the era of the lavish production shows, with fabulous costumes, extravagant stage sets, and lots of special effects.

Today, there's a resurgence of big-name entertainment, with showrooms like **MGM Grand's Hollywood Theatre** (702/891-7777), the newly renovated **Aladdin Theater for the Performing Arts** (702/474-4000), **Mandalay Bay's Events Center** (702/632-7580), **Bally's Celebrity Room** (702/739-4567), and **Orleans Showroom** at the Orleans Hotel/Casino (702/365-7075) featuring top-drawer stars. When Mandalay Bay's Events Center opened in 1999, Luciano Pavarotti was the featured performer, and since that time the venue has played host to such cultural attractions as tenor Andrea Bocelli and the Russian Symphony Orchestra.

Despite the renaissance of headliner shows, the long-run production shows have been so popular that it looks as if they will also continue to be an important part of the entertainment scene.

In the next chapter, we tell you about the production shows that are suitable for families to attend together—shows with long runs that promise to be ongoing. This chapter is primarily devoted to entertainments with a shorter stage life—superstar performances, concerts, plays, and such.

Some of the headliners put on shows that are acceptable for children; others definitely do not. Among the entertainers who appear frequently and whose shows most every family would find suitable are Bill Cosby, Reba McEntire, Wayne Newton, and Alabama.

The minimum admittance age for children depends upon the show. Ticket pricing does, too. And though the entertainers usually perform in hotel/casino showrooms, they also appear in venues not connected with the gaming industry. If you're planning to attend a casino show of any kind that's presented in a showroom, buy your tickets in advance and plan to arrive at least forty-five minutes to an hour before a show begins, because seating lines can be very long (many tickets specify seating time). When the entertainment takes place in a non-casino venue and you hold reserved seat tickets, it is not necessary to arrive as early if you walk or take a cab, but you should allow plenty of time for parking if you drive to the show.

In addition to the superstar appearances, diversions such as ice skating shows, traveling troupes of performers from various parts of the world, and international gymnastics competitions are frequently on the Las Vegas entertainment calendar. For example, one ice rink was constructed at the Fremont Experience for a 1996 Christmas TV spectacular featuring Nancy Kerrigan, and another one was built on the Strip especially for another ice show that showcased several top skaters, including Tara Lipinsky and Michele Kwan.

More than two dozen venues, in addition to those located in

casinos, provide the stages and spaces for the city's entertainments. Five of the performance centers are quite large—the **MGM Grand Garden Arena** with 15,200 seats (702/891-1111); **Thomas & Mack Center** on the University of Nevada–Las Vegas campus with 18,500 seats (702/895-3761); **Sam Boyd's Silver Bowl** (Boulder Highway at Russell Road; 702/895-3200) can seat 126,000 in a concert configuration; **Mandalay Bay Events Center** has 12,000 seats; and **Aladdin's Theater for the Performing Arts** (3667 Las Vegas Boulevard S.; 702/736-0111), 7,000. Most major concerts take place at these sites, four of which—the MGM Grand Garden Arena, Thomas & Mack Center, the Silver Bowl, and Mandalay Bay Events Center—also host various athletic events.

The **Artemus W. Ham Concert Hall** and the **Judy Bayley Theatre,** both part of the UNLV Performing Arts Center (on the university campus at 4505 S. Maryland Parkway; 702/895-3535), seat 1,885 and 556, respectively; the auditorium at **Las Vegas Academy of International Studies, Performing and Visual Arts** (315 S. 7th Street; 702/799-7800) seats 1,500; and the **Cashman Field Theatre** accommodates 1,940. Although the city has several outdoor amphitheaters that hold from 500 to 3,000 people, most of the other indoor performance venues seat between 150 and 300.

Many of the large auditorium performances are one-night affairs, especially those featuring rock bands. Others are annual events.

Beyond the Neon

Since Las Vegas is a university town, a larger than average segment of the population is interested in cultural events. In addition, many of the performers in the production shows have been classically trained and become weary of performing the same old routines every night. So on their time off, they're involved in theater repertory and Actors Equity-type groups. As a result, almost every evening a Broadway play is being presented, a ballet performed, or some other type of cultural event is going on somewhere in the city.

In addition to UNLV, the City of Las Vegas and Clark County sponsor impressive arrays of cultural programs and events each year. Call 702/229-6713 to receive a bi-monthly calendar.

Add to these performances the fact that there are some ninety not-for-profit arts and cultural organizations in Las Vegas, many of which mount performances, and you can see why the city's slogan—Entertainment Capital of the World—doesn't refer only to its extravaganzas presented on the Strip.

Not only are most of these non-neon performances of outstanding quality, they won't put a strain on the family vacation budget. That's because many of the presentations are underwritten by groups such as the Nevada State Council on the Arts, public radio station KNPR, the Musicians' Union, and the Music Performance Trust Fund. Also, city- and county-sponsored events are often free.

More than four hundred events are held each year in the university's Performing Arts Center. **Artemus W. Ham Hall** (4505 S. Maryland Parkway; 702/895-3801); bus 109, 201, or 302) and the **Nevada Opera Theatre** (702/699-9775) present performances of such classics as *Madame Butterfly*. The **Nevada Symphony Orchestra** (702/792-4337) also performs there. Many of the symphony's musicians earn their livings by playing six nights a week on the Strip. In addition to its appearances at Ham Hall, the Nevada Symphony plays several outdoor concerts—including the July Picnic Pops—at Hills Park in Summerlin (a development in the northwest corner of the city).

On other nights at Ham Hall, the **Charles Vanda Master Series** presents the likes of the Bolshoi Ballet Ensemble and London's Royal Philharmonic Orchestra. **Nevada Dance Theatre** (702/895–2787), the only professional ballet company in Nevada, performs such works as the ballet version of *Dracula* at the Judy Bayley Theatre (in the Performing Arts Center; 702/739-3838).

The company, which often utilizes the services of world-renowned choreographers, presents four programs during its September–May season, including the traditional *Nutcracker* in December. Most of the performances that are sponsored by the City of Las Vegas take place at four different sites—the **Sammy Davis, Jr. Festival Plaza** at Lorenzi Park (3333 W. Washington Avenue; 702/229-6297), **Reed Whipple Cultural Center** (821 Las Vegas Boulevard N.; 702/229-6211), **Charleston Heights Art Center** (800 S. Brush; 702/229-6383), and **West Las Vegas Arts Center** (947 W. Lake Mead Boulevard; 702/229-4800). The performers are an eclectic mix—a Peruvian classical guitarist, a Zydeco accordian player, the Maxwell Street Klezmer Band, the American Tap Dance Orchestra, and the National Theater of the Deaf are only a few of those who have appeared under the city's auspices.

One city-sponsored group that's especially popular with youngsters is **Rainbow Company Children's Theater** (821 Las Vegas Boulevard N.; 702/229-6553). Actors, both children and adults, are chosen by annual audition. Variety of programming is illustrated by the five productions of the group's 1997–1998 season, which included a lighthearted musical fantasy called *No One Will Marry a Princess with a Tree Growing Out of Her Head* and *The Crane Wife,* a Japanese folktale with symbolic movement, ceremonial masks, and percussive music. There's also a city-sponsored **Children's Summer Concert Series** (Charleston Heights Art Center; 702/229-6383). The series includes an array of performances, such as a puppet theater production of *Thimbelina*, folk music from around the world, and a multiethnic storytelling session.

In March, the annual **"Search for Talent"** competition, which is free, features youngsters from the ages of six to eighteen. Held on three Saturdays during the month, more than a hundred contestants, divided into age groups, present their acts at Reed Whipple Cultural Center. Other competitions, such as the Country Music Oranization of America's annual **American**

Eagle Awards Talent Search are held from time to time in the city and publicized in the weekly events magazines.

Many of the city's most delightful entertainments are held outdoors, taking advantage of Las Vegas's fine evenings. The **Melodrama in the Parks** appears at various city parks in June. An outdoor **Family Film Festival** (Jaycee Park, St. Louis and Eastern Avenues; 702/229-6211) takes place on Thursday nights in July and August. **The Las Vegas Blues Society** sponsors free outdoor "blues picnics" in spring and fall, featuring local bands.

Each July, the county sponsors **Jazz in the Park** at Clark County Government Center Amphitheater downtown (702/455-8200). The amphitheater is also used for noontime brown-bag concerts and other county-sponsored performances such as a recent evening of traditional Celtic music. The Las Vegas Summer Band, composed of professional musicians, music educators, and students, also presents several outdoor band concerts at various venues throughout the city.

The **Nevada Humanities Committee** (800/382-5023) presents events showcasing music, poetry, storytelling, dance, and other art forms at various halls and theaters, and is responsible for bringing live performances to school children around the state.

Las Vegas Little Theatre (702/362-7996) and **New West Theatre Company** (702/876-8022) provide drama, comedy, and Broadway musicals for the theatergoing public. Prices vary with the group and the production, but are mostly in the $8.00 to $12.50 range, with discounts for students. Among the most popular dramatic performances each year are the **Nevada Shakespeare in the Park** productions (702/458-8855) in late September—in fact, **Shakespeare in the Park** is Las Vegas's largest annual cultural event. Professional Shakespearean companies put on the plays (1997's was *The Tempest*), whose backdrops—along with the park's natural setting—add to the experience. "Green Shows," which include mimes, madrigal singers, and jugglers, precede the performances.

The city's ethnic organizations frequently put on special entertainment, sometimes in conjunction with a festival; others as stand-alone events. It might be a performance by Hawaiian singers or Japanese drummers; black gospel choirs or Basque dancers. But whatever ethnic group they represent, the colorful performances add to their audiences' appreciation of that group's culture.

To find out what's going on while you're in town, check out the weekly/monthly entertainment magazines that are available at most hotel concierge or bell desks. The Friday and Saturday editions of the *Las Vegas Review Journal* are also good sources of information.

The children's most lasting memories of Las Vegas entertainment, however, will be of walking down the Strip after dark looking at the nighttime neon display. Don't worry too much about the hawkers distributing girlie brochures. They don't hand them to family groups, and the younger children will probably be too interested in looking at the bright lights to notice. When you drive or take a cab or the bus, the heavy traffic will give you just that much more time to see the sights.

If you don't have a hotel room facing on the Strip, you'll probably want to go to the top of Stratosphere or have dinner at the top of the Rio, since the view of the valley lights is spectacular.

CHAPTER 9

Reviewing the Shows

Las Vegas *is* the Entertainment Capital of the World. No doubt about it. And the big production shows generate a great deal of the entertainment excitement. Since these shows cost millions of dollars to produce, they are performed nightly for several years and become the trademark entertainment of the hotel/casinos where they are presented.

Many of the Las Vegas productions are big on bare breasts and behinds, though they're usually tastefully exposed. Most of the productions with partial nudity exclude people under the age of twenty-one. Comedy shows, however, are less likely to have age requirements, and comedians whose material on TV is squeaky clean can be positively raunchy once they hit the Las Vegas stages.

Despite the fact that many Las Vegas shows are definitely adult entertainment, more than a dozen of them qualify as suitable for family viewing, at least as far as most parents are concerned.

Nonetheless, even if there's no minimum age limit, use good judgment in determining whether younger children are up to sitting still and remaining quiet for more than an hour (most shows last about ninety minutes).

The Shows in Review

The information that follows includes only those shows that the average family will find acceptable. Even so, this should be used merely as a guide, as scripts can change and new segments be added or deleted from the production shows. Since differences in family tastes and values vary so greatly, we've attempted to alert readers to any aspects of a particular show they might not want their children to experience. Remember, too, that reviews are highly subjective. A show that knocks our socks off won't necessarily leave everyone with the same feeling.

At the top of our list is *Mystere* at Treasure Island (702/894-7722). The show is among the most imaginative productions playing anywhere, and children seem to enjoy it just as much as adults. Featuring the Cirque du Soleil troupe, which was formed in 1984 by a group of young French-Canadian street performers, the show is technically a circus. But it is totally unlike the three-ring kind.

From the opening big bang of a Taiko drum ensemble, the show's aura of mystery is enhanced by exotic costuming, inventive lighting, and live music—best described, perhaps, as classic–New Age. One group of acrobats look like elves from outer space, with frilled antennas sprouting from the tops of their skullcaps, pointed noses, and round bellies; another group is clad in one-piece helmet-to-toe leotards of tomato red.

Top Russian trapeze artists trained for fourteen months perfecting their act for *Mystere*. A show-stopper called "Vis Versa" features two men who perform incredible balancing feats while on a rotating circular platform. Acrobats clamber up and down Chinese poles. Others perform suspended by bungee cords overhead.

The only members of the eighty-performer cast who speak (or babble) are the two comics—an oversized baby in rompers and an unusually amusing character called Monsieur Benny Le Grand—and the ringmaster.

The 1,525-seat Cirque du Soleil Theater, which was custom-built for the show, features an elaborately painted dome and catwalks beneath it on which the musicians are stationed. The curtainless stage and three-tier seating ensure that the musicians and singers are in full view of the audience at all times. Among the very best seats in the house are those in the low numbers from Row D to Row G.

Shows begin at 7:30 P.M. and 10:30 P.M., Wednesday through Sunday. Tickets cost $88 for adults and children (prices include tax).

While *Mystere* is a "one of it's kind" production, *Lance Burton: Master Magician* (Monte Carlo Hotel/Casino, 800/311-8999 or 702/730-7000) isn't the only sleight-of-hand artist plying his artistic trade in Las Vegas. But he is undeniably the best. In fact, he's among the most accomplished magicians in the world.

Burton not only transforms silk handkerchiefs into doves, he produces a gaggle of geese seemingly out of nowhere. He pours champagne into a glass suspended in air, beheads a court jester, puts his arms around a showgirl who immediately disappears. He levitates. Frees himself from a straightjacket. Makes a full-size roadster vanish.

In a segment of each show, Burton invites a youngster in the audience to volunteer as his assistant and sometimes winds up with one to two dozen children onstage (they all get to stay there until that part of the performance is over).

Top-notch comedian, Michael Goudeau is a standout as Burton's bumbling stagehand. One of Goudeau's most memorable feats involves juggling a lighted torch, a bowling ball, and a chainsaw.

The show takes place in a 1,274-seat Victorian-style showroom, which cost $27 million and was designed especially for Burton's production (the magician signed a thirteen-year contract with Monte Carlo during the construction phase of the hotel/casino).

Showtimes are Tuesday through Saturday at 7:30 P.M. and

10:30 P.M. Balcony seats cost $54.00; main floor and mezzanine, $59.95. Ticket prices include taxes and tip, and the show is considered the best value-for-money production in town.

The plot of $45 million *EFX* is weak. The acting and music aren't especially memorable. But the costuming and special effects in the show at MGM Grand (800/929-1111 or 702/891-7777) are among the most spectacular you'll see anywhere (EFX is show-biz slang for special effects).

Divided into ten acts, the show stars Rick Springfield. Springfield rocks and rolls his way through the production as a busboy who has lost his power of imagination and must undergo a series of fairly illogical adventures orchestrated by the Masters of Magic, Spirits, Time, and Laughter. To energize the production, rock and roll was substituted for the show's original music.

Stunningly realistic backdrops portray everything from nineteenth-century London to the futuristic caves of the barbaric Morlocks. The special effects highlight of the show comes in Act Four, when Springfield is sent to Camelot where he becomes King Arthur, meets Merlin the Magician, and confronts enormous, fire-breathing dragons.

Equally awe-inspiring, however, is the skill of the Flying Kaganovich troupe, who appear in Act Five, "Intergalactic Circus of Wonders." Probably the most skilled aerialists performing today, members of the troupe execute heart-stopping maneuvers as they catapult through the air.

Eighty-five thousand watts of state-of-the-art stereo amplifiers drive three hundred loudspeakers placed about the theater—some of them under the seats. Eighteen different kinds of lights consume enough power to light 1,440 average-size homes.

The show runs nightly, Tuesday through Saturday, in MGM Grand's 1,700-seat Grand Theatre. Performances are at 7:30 P.M. and 10:30 P.M. Tickets cost $55 or $75 for preferred seating; $40 for children five to twelve years old. All prices include tax. Though children under the age of five aren't permitted to attend, older children who are sensitive to sudden noises and scary creatures that are larger than life may find the production frightening.

Water is the centerpiece of the Cirque du Soleil fantasy called *"O"* (the show gets its name from the pronunciation of the French word for water, *eau*). The production plays in the $70 million theater at Bellagio (702/796-9999), which was custom-built for it.

The show begins with sixteen pairs of feet dancing above the water's surface in an upside-down water ballet. Throughout the performance, the water levels change with the aid of five hi-tech hydraulic lifts. Sometimes it is knee-deep; at other times there's only a trace of it on the stage. During a dramatic segment, an aerialist does a swan dive into a twenty-five-foot-deep pool. And there are scenes when the stage is completely dry.

Like all Cirque du Soleil productions, *"O"* puts a new spin on the traditional circus acts. All the equipment used is traditional circus apparatus, innovatively modified. Costuming is as imaginative as you will find anywhere. Original music composed for each production is played by top quality musicians whose costumes are as fanciful as those of the performers.

The themes, also typical of Cirque productions, are of everyman—hope, despair; happiness, sorrow; longing, fulfillment. It is definitely not necessary, however, to completely understand the symbolism in order to enjoy the performance. Tickets cost from $99 to $121.

Lord of the Dance (New York-New York; 702/740-6815) takes Irish step dancing to a new level. The lilting music is definitely Celtic, and the dancers—true to tradition—keep their upper bodies erect and literally motionless. But the configurations of their routines and of their footwork definitely go beyond that you'll see in the Emerald Isle.

Created by dancer-choreographer Michael Flatley, the former lead dancer of *Riverdance,* the show is a mix of ensemble numbers and performances by the troupe's stars. The entertainment includes hauntingly beautiful instrumental numbers, too, featuring a violin and flute as well as bagpipes.

Especially charming is a number in which Good (she wears white) and Evil (dressed in red) vie with their fancy footwork to win the Lord of the Dance. Don't be surprised to see your youngsters step dance as you stroll down the Strip after seeing the show. Tickets are $59 Tuesday through Thursday; $68 Friday and Saturday; and $50 for the Saturday matinee.

Siegfried & Roy in Theatre Mirage (702/792-7777) at Mirage is one of the most expensive shows ($89.35 for admission, two drinks, souvenir program, gratuity, and tax) in Las Vegas, other than the headliner performances of stars like Barbra Streisand. It's a spectacular show—no doubt about that—with elaborate staging, tigers that vanish before your eyes, and showgirls adorned with baubles, bangles, and beads. People rave about it.

Our take on the show, however, is that although Siegfried & Roy's Secret Garden at the Mirage is a delight (see chapter 6), the show at times seems repetitive and boring—perhaps once you've seen a white tiger disappear, you don't have to see it happen again and again. For some visitors, however, no trip to Las Vegas will be considered complete without the experience. If, on the other hand, members of your family are not fond of animal shows or magicians who do a lot of posing, choose another production. Shows are presented Friday through Tuesday, at 7:30 P.M. and 11 P.M.

While the nostalgia aspect of *Legends in Concert* at the Imperial Palace (702/794-3261) will appeal to parents, many youngsters may not have a clue as to who some of the superstars are supposed to be. But on the other hand, they won't be as critical about whether the Elvis impersonator really looks and sounds like Elvis. Among the show numbers are the Blues Brothers (Eric Martin and Carmen Romano), ripping through "Rawhide," and Madonna (Kimberly Goltry), pleading "Don't Cry for Me Argentina."

The show goes on in the smoke-free Imperial Theater at 7:30 P.M. and 10:30 P.M., Monday through Saturday. Tickets cost $34.50 for adults; $19.50 for children twelve and under. Readily available discount coupons take nearly 10 percent off the price of an adult ticket. There's no minimum attendance age.

Caesars Magical Empire at Caesars Palace (800/445-4544 or 702/731-7333) combines dining and technology, while relying on the Las Vegas favorite theme of the past few years—magic. The experience begins as diners, divided into groups of twenty-four, are escorted into the Chamber of Destiny near the attraction's entrance. There guests are given a fictional history of Caesars Magical Empire before they are transported underground by environmental illusion.

After a short walk through the "catacombs," participants arrive at one of ten "Dining Chambers of the Gods." Throughout dinner, entertainment is provided by a sorcerer's apprentice, and food is carried in by female servants in white toga-style gowns. Entree choices include veal, chicken, salmon, and a vegetarian dish, served with salad, twice-baked potatoes, fresh vegetables, rolls, dessert, and beverage.

After dinner, guests can wander at will throughout the area adjacent to the dining chamber. Centerpiece of the area is Sanctum Secorum, where the big event is the "Lumineria Show" and visit by the host wizard, Ceronomous. At the Secret Pagoda Theatre, magicians perform close-up magic in an intimate seventy-two-seat setting. At the larger Sultan's Palace Theatre, emphasis is on grand-scale illusions. Free Lumineria Shows from 11:00 A.M. to 4:00 P.M. daily offer a sneak preview, which may help you decide whether your family will enjoy the Magical Empire experience. Dinner seatings begin at 4:30 P.M. Tickets cost $75.50.

The *King Arthur's Tournament* dinner show is presented in King Arthur's Arena at Excalibur (702/597-7600), a nine-hundred-seat, theater-in-the-round-style showroom. Counters in front of each row of seats provide places for the dinner items, all of which can be eaten with the hands. Soup is served in porringers; along with a small chicken, broccoli, half of a baked potato, and a roll on a platter. There are cupcakes for dessert. The eating process is somewhat messy, despite the fact that each diner is provided with a damp towel.

After dinner, the King Arthur's Tournament portion of the show begins. An original musical production adapted to the legend of King Arthur, it takes audiences back to the jousting tournaments of the Middle Ages.

The story begins as a young boy gallops his horse around the arena and encounters Merlin the Magician, who transports him back to medieval days and transforms him into the White Knight of Kent. The White Knight meets King Arthur and Queen Guinevere, then joins the other knights in the tournament. Good ultimately triumphs over evil as the White Knight defeats the treacherous Dark Knight and wins the princess's hand.

Various entertainments, including an excellent circus-type trick-riding exhibition, follow the tournament. The entire production, from dinner to the end of the show, lasts about an hour and a half.

Shows are presented nightly at 6:00 P.M. and 8:30 P.M. The $29.95 ticket price includes the dinner show, tax, and gratuities. There's no age limit on who can attend King Arthur's Tournament.

There's a four-year age minimum for Stratosphere's *American Superstars* (Friday–Wednesday, 7:00 P.M. and 10 P.M.; $29.95 for adults; $22.95 for children, including tax); and children must be at least six years old to get into *Viva Las Vegas* (Monday–Saturday, 2:00 P.M. and 4 P.M.), also at Stratosphere (800/99-TOWER or 702/380-7711; $11.95 plus tax).

As the prices of production show and superstar extravaganza tickets have escalated, several hotel/casinos have inaugurated less expensive shows, which are presented in the afternoon. Added to the handful of afternoon shows already on the entertainment scene, these newcomers provide a greater number of options. They aren't as lavish, perhaps, as the evening production shows, but are for the most part good value for money spent.

In his show, *Michael Holly* (Sahara; 702/737–2111) does some comedy and a little magic, too. Most of all, he juggles—bowling balls, chain saws, M&M's, apples, hatchets, and bones. The show price is $12.95, but with an easy-to-find discount coupon, it's $6.55.

The *Mac King Comedy Magic Show* (Harrah's; 702/369-5222) is a one-man performance, but the man is a pro—both as a comic and a magician. Tickets cost $16.45, but people who signed up for Harrah's Total Rewards slot club in 2001 were given two free tickets to the show (not really free, however, because each ticket-holder was required to buy a $5.95 drink).

Every afternoon except Friday, the *Illusionary Magic of Rick Thomas* plays in the Tropicana (702/739-2411). Thomas, who with his sister was at one time a Junior Amateur Ballroom Dancing champion, presents a kid-pleasing show that incorporates a lot of music and dancing, as well as birds and animals. It's not a big-budget show like many of the others in Las Vegas, but the price is a lot less, too. Tickets for the two afternoon shows, scheduled for 2:00 P.M. and 4:00 P.M., cost $12.95, but widely distributed discount coupons can cut the cost by as much as $3.00 per person.

The free *Bird Man of Las Vegas*, featuring Joe Krathwoke and his fine feathered friends (Flamingo Hilton; 702/733-3333) is presented at 11 A.M., 12:30 P.M., and 2 P.M. daily except Thursday.

The King in Concert at Elvis-A-Rama (702/794-8200; see chapter 6) stars Tim Welch, who looks the part as he sings Elvis favorites to taped music.

Probably the least expensive show in town and one that will make little kids happy is *Dixie Dooley's Magic Show*, presented at 4:00 P.M. and 5:30 P.M. Tuesday through Sunday in the Lighthouse Showroom of the Holiday Inn Boardwalk (702/730-3194). Tickets cost $8.95, adults; $5, children.

Superstar Spectaculars and Limited Run Productions

The newly renovated Aladdin Theater for the Performing Arts, which has been incorporated into the new Aladdin Resort, is the venue for Broadway musicals and other big theatrical events. Since it opened in August 2000, *Les Miserables, Riverdance, Fosse,* and *Fame: The Musical* have been among the productions presented on its stage. Other headline performers and attractions have included Sarah Brightman and *Forever Swing: The Big Band Musical Review.* Las Vegas trend-watchers see this sort of entertainment becoming more important in the next few years.

To maximize the experience at whatever shows you decide to attend, look at a seating chart before you buy your tickets in order to get the best seats available in your price range. Also, if the ticket price you're quoted doesn't include tax and tip, be sure to factor in the 17 percent tax (10 percent entertainment tax plus 7 percent state tax) as well as a 10 to 15 percent gratuity. If you order your tickets for any sort of an event—showroom production, cultural performance, or athletic event—from a booking agency, there will be a booking fee (generally about $2) added to the price of each ticket. In some situations, a booking agency may be your only choice, but usually you can get tickets directly from the box office.

When you have the option of buying a ticket that does not include the meal at a dinner show, you'll probably be ahead of the game if you buy the show-only ticket. Few Las Vegas showroom dinners get rave reviews.

CHAPTER 10

Day Trips and Excursions

One of Las Vegas's best-kept secrets is that it is close to so many other interesting places. After all, the city's dominant group of advertisers—casinos—aren't going to shout about anything that will tell customers there's more to do than pushing the slot machine spin buttons and gathering around the "21" tables.

The unheralded truth is that Glitz City is a natural starting point for trips to lakes, the desert, and some of the most impressive geologic formations in the world.

Las Vegas is only a half-hour's drive from the California and Arizona borders and not much more than an hour away from Utah, so we have included a few of the most spectacular excursions to those states. The farthest away can be reached in five and a half hours by car (forty minutes by air), but most of them are much closer.

Among the most gratifying day trips for families are those to **Red Rock Canyon,** about a thirty-minute drive from the Strip (follow West Charleston Boulevard—Highway 159—until you reach the well-marked turnoff). Rising three thousand feet on the eastern edge of the Spring Mountains, the Red Rock escarpment resulted from violent geologic shifting thousands of years ago. The formations are especially lovely in the light of sunrise and sunset.

Greenery, including Ponderosa pines, decorates the canyons, cracks, crannies, and crevices. Mountain streams and waterfalls splash and tumble in winter and spring. Nature lovers might well want to poke about Red Rock during their entire Las Vegas stay.

To view the striated formation in all its glory, stop first at Red Rock Vista, about a mile past the highway turnoff. A short distance farther along the scenic thirteen-mile loop road (open from 7:00 A.M. until dusk) at the Visitor Center (8:30 A.M. to 4:30 P.M.), you can pick up a free map of the park and buy a topographical map, both of which are essential if you plan to do any extensive hiking.

While you're at the center, take time to browse around the bookstore, stocked with reading material about flora, fauna, geology, and other nature-related subjects as well as a great selection of Western-themed books for children. There's also a small museum, with stuffed animals, geology exhibits, and other displays that explain the area's natural history (listening wands are available at no charge). A viewing terrace (with telescopes) outside the museum will give you close-ups of the surrounding formations.

Families who like to hike can choose from an array of routes, ranging from easy one- and two-mile jaunts to the strenuous fourteen-mile round-trip to the top of the escarpment. All sixteen hikes are described in a free brochure called "Red Rock Canyon National Conservation Area Hiking" that's available at the Visitor Center.

One of the most popular treks is the Moenkope Loop, an easy two-mile trail through cottontop barrel cactus, creosote plants, blackbrush, and yucca. The six-mile Lamadre Spring hike follows a trail to the spring, which provides the water supply for bighorn sheep and other wildlife that inhabit the area. It's classed as moderately strenuous.

Ice Box Canyon, which is two and a half miles round-trip, is moderately difficult and involves some rock scrambling. This is a good choice for warmer days because, as its name implies, the canyon is cooler than surrounding areas.

Another choice is the Children's Discovery Trail to Lost Creek with a free workbook/guide that each young hiker can write in and color. The book not only describes the numbered points of interest along the way, but also helps develop the reader's powers of observation.

Any child who wants to become a Junior Ranger can also ask for a Discovery Book. When the workbook pages have been successfully completed, the child is awarded a Ranger Badge and certificate.

If you spend your Red Rock time driving the loop, be sure to stop occasionally to enjoy the natural wonders around you. With binoculars, you may be able to spot bighorn sheep, gray foxes, bobcats, and wild burros at the higher elevations. Even if you don't see any of the larger animals, you're sure to see squirrels and a whole bird book full of orioles, tanagers, wrens, hummingbirds, and other species.

Just down Highway 159 from Red Rock Canyon is **Spring Mountain Ranch State Park.** Centerpiece of the park is the ranch formerly owned by Vera Krupp of Germany's foremost munitions dynasty and later by Howard Hughes. Park rangers conduct a number of activities throughout the year, and on summer evenings outdoor productions of such musical comedies as *My Fair Lady* and *Seven Brides for Seven Brothers* are presented by a little theater group.

Instead of returning to Las Vegas by the same route, you might drive on to **Bonnie Springs** (see chapter 6) and then on to **Blue Diamond.** There's not much to see—the road sign that announces the town says "Pop: Low, Alt: High"—but you'll find a pretty little park across the street from Blue Diamond's only store, Village Market and Mercantile. It's only about twenty minutes from the park to Las Vegas Boulevard south of the Strip.

Hitting the Heights

Mt. Charleston, forty-five miles northwest of the city, is one of the biggest surprises in the Las Vegas orbit—especially in winter, when people are shussing down the slopes on skis. It's an ideal day-trip destination in summer, too, when temperatures on the valley floor sizzle (the mountain is usually twenty to thirty degrees cooler than it is outdoors on the Strip.

Whether you explore the park by car, on skis (facilities include three chair lifts, which take passengers to more than forty acres of bunny, intermediate, and expert slopes), foot, or bicycle, you'll want to plan on eating outdoors as Mt. Charleston is one of Nevada's best picnic spots. You'll find tables and other picnic facilities at Cathedral Rock, Old Mill, Robber's Roost, and Deer Creek.

Experienced backpackers will enjoy the challenge of climbing to the summit of Mt. Charleston (11,918 feet). There are two routes to the top. One begins in Lee's Canyon and is an eleven-mile-hike round-trip. The trailhead for the second (nine miles) is at Cathedral Rock. To avoid coming back in the dark, most hikers make at least one overnight camp. It's also important to stay on marked trails, especially at the higher elevations.

Less experienced hikers can choose from a variety of trails, including one to the majestic Cathedral Rock and another to Deer Creek. One of the most delightful hikes in springtime is the four-hour trek to Mary Jane and Big Falls in upper Kyle Canyon. The ranger station, located in Kyle Canyon, is the place to obtain maps and information about the area (702/872-5486).

For the ultimate in driving pleasure, leave the car windows down so that you can smell as well as look at the vegetation of the different climatic zones you pass through on your climb up the mountain. Joshua trees, yucca—and desert wildflowers in the spring—carpet the valley floor. When you reach five thousand feet, you'll see piñon pine, juniper, sage, and rabbit brush.

Another thousand feet higher and you'll be in mountain mahogany, ponderosa pine, and blueberry territory, with springtime blossoms of such species as penstemon. Though the paved road ends at 7,500 feet, you can look up to see the tortured branches of five-thousand-year-old bristlecone pine, believed by some botanists to be the oldest plant species existing today.

Permanent Mt. Charleston residents include several hundred people who commute each day to Las Vegas, and Palmer chipmunks, which are found nowhere else in the world. And though you most likely won't see them, coyotes, fox, bighorn sheep, elk, deer, bobcats, and cougar live there, too.

Families with well-developed leg muscles may want to explore Red Rock Canyon and Mt. Charleston by bicycle. McGhies (4503 West Sahara; 702/252-8077 and 3310 East Flamingo; 702/433-1120) rents bikes for $25 to $45 per day, depending on the kind of bike. Escape the City Streets (8221 W. Charleston Boulevard; 702/596-2953) both rent bikes and conducts tours.

Mountain T Ranch on State Route 157 (702/656-8025) offers two-hour-and-twenty-minute trail rides in the Mt. Charleston foothills for $30 per rider, while trail rides that originate at Bonnie Springs Motel on State Route 159 (702/875-4400) last one hour, cost $20, and go into the Red Rock area.

An Orchard Oasis

If your family likes to go on fruit-picking expeditions, head for **Gilcrease Orchards** (7800 N. Tenaya Way) fifteen miles north of downtown Las Vegas. Plums and peaches are ripe in July; peaches, pears, and apples, in August; apples and pears in September. The fruit costs about thirty to forty cents a pound. The orchard is open daily from 7:00 A.M. until noon. The easiest way to get there is by going north on U.S. 95, east on Ann Road, making a quick left, and then turning right on Tenaya. Call 702/645-1126 and you'll get a recorded message telling what kind of fruits are ready to pick.

During the Jurassic period, Mother Nature was busy making red sandstone formations out of great dunes of sand in the Las Vegas area. Through the next hundred million years, wind and water carved the six-mile-long depression that is now **Valley of Fire State Park.** Located fifty-five miles northeast of the city (take U.S. 15 north, turning off at exit 75, Route 169), the area is a fantasy of domes, pinnacles, and spires in colors of crimson, scarlet, deep purple, brilliant orange, and the palest shades of pink.

At the visitor center (702/645-1126)—your logical first stop—maps, trail guides, and the books on the region's history, geology, and ecology that are for sale can make an enjoyable excursion educational as well. Exhibits at the center explain the natural forces that created the park's geological wonders. And don't miss the chance to get a close-up look at the endangered tortoise species.

The Valley of Fire has been inhabited by humans at various times for more than five thousand years—some sources say twenty thousand—and the marks they have left upon it are among the park's most interesting features. Members of each succeeding tribal group, from the Fremont culture to the Anasazi, the Yuma, and the more recent Paiutes, left messages incised upon the rocks.

Some of these petroglyphs served as road maps, perhaps others were billboards or signs to attract the attention of subsequent travelers. The rocks also contain religious symbols and figures from everyday life of hundreds and thousands of years ago.

The best views of the petroglyphs are at Atlatl Rock and in Petroglyph Canyon. Many of the carvings on the rock depict an ancient spear-throwing stick called the *atlatl* in one of the Aztec dialects. They are believed to predate A.D. 500, when the bow and arrow replaced the *atlatl* in southern Nevada.

The park's most unusual formation is Elephant Rock, said to resemble the mammoths that roamed the earth many thousands of years ago. The Beehive Rocks are symmetrically weathered boulders that look like giant hives. As you might imagine, the more inaccessible areas of the park have been popular with directors of film and TV westerns, since they don't have to contend with modern-day nuisances such as power lines and telephone poles.

It takes only fifteen or twenty minutes to drive through the valley, but you'll probably want to get out and stretch your legs. Self-guided trails range from those that are less than a mile and easy to walk to longer ones that are more difficult. One of the shorter self-guided trails leads to Mouse's Tank, a series of catch basins named for a turn-of-the-century Native American called Mouse, who was either holed up there hiding from the law or stayed there after he was banished from the tribe, depending upon which version of the story you hear. Two other trails lead to 225-million-year-old petrified logs.

Throughout the park, the rock catchments (also called tanks or *tinajas*) that collect water when it rains are where you are most likely to spot the birds, reptiles, mammals, and insects that inhabit the area. Awe inspiring as the Valley of Fire is, it's not a trip that you'll want to make in the dead of summer, when temperatures are egg-frying hot.

Twelve miles north of the Valley of Fire State Park in the little town of Overton, the **Lost City Museum** (721 S. Moapa Valley Boulevard; 702/397-2193) contains one of the most complete collections of early Pueblo Indian artifacts in the Southwest. Museum displays span the period of the desert culture of ten thousand years ago, when man hunted now-extinct species such as the mammoth and the ground sloth, to the Mormon farmers who first settled the Valley in 1865.

In addition to the exhibits, several Pueblo-style houses of wattle and daub have been reconstructed on their foundations, and plants used by the early Indians are part of the surrounding landscape.

Engineering Par Excellence

A half hour south of Las Vegas on U.S. 93, Hoover Dam is counted among the seven engineering wonders of the world. For eons, the Colorado River had periodically run amok as it raced along its way to the Gulf of California.

Lands flooded, topsoil eroded, crops shriveled, and cattle died. So in 1931, construction began on the first arch-gravity-type dam ever built. Nonstop work on the dam was a twenty-four-hour-a-day project until 1935, when the 726-foot-high dam was dedicated by President Franklin D. Roosevelt. At that time, however, it was christened Boulder, rather than Hoover, Dam.

Since that time, more than 37 million visitors have toured the massive facility, which annually produces enough electricity to provide half a million homes with power for one year. It also furnishes water to agricultural enterprises and cities downriver.

Guided tours of the dam, which actually take you inside the structure, are offered from 8:45 A.M. to 5:45 P.M. daily (8:00 A.M. to 6:00 P.M. Memorial Day through Labor Day). Admission is $10 for adults; $8 for seniors over sixty-five; $3 for juniors seven to sixteen years; and free for children under the age of seven. There is also a hard-hat tour that costs $25 per person (children under the age of seven are not permitted to take the tour and participants must wear closed-toe shoes). Viewing stations on either side of the river offer dramatic views of the gigantic concrete structure.

If the tour inspires you to learn even more about the dam's construction, go to the **Boulder City Dam Museum** (444 Hotel Plaza, Boulder City; 702/294-1988) to look at photo exhibits and other dam memorabilia. Admission is $1 for adults; $.50 for children under twelve. A historical walking tour goes past points of interest in this town, which came into being to take care of the dam builders' needs.

When the Colorado River was backed up by Hoover Dam, it created the largest man-made body of water in the United States, with 550 miles of freshwater shoreline. Lake Mead is starkly beautiful, rather than pretty, with rock formations forming the backdrop for its aquamarine waters.

If you've decided to rent a houseboat (see chapter 2), you'll be able to spend some time relaxing in a deck chair or throwing out a fishing line into the water. If you do the latter, be sure to get a Nevada fishing license. A nonresident permit costs $7 for one day and $2 for each additional day. A license that is good for one year costs $51. Children sixteen and under don't need a license. Anyone over the age of sixteen who fishes for trout also needs to buy a $5 trout stamp.

When you stay there, you can grill your catch of the day, roast marshmallows, swim, read books, and go into Las Vegas only when you feel in need of neon. Another option is to follow the designated underwater scuba trail at Boulder Beach. Or you might want to rent jet skis, a kayak, or a skiboat and water skis at one of the six marinas on the lake.

Anyone who can drive a car can operate a houseboat, so you might want to explore some of the more interesting spots along the lake's shoreline, including the Bat Caves and Lower Granite Gorge on the Colorado River.

If you haven't hired a houseboat, you can still enjoy Lake Mead's special places and pleasures. Boulder Beach is a gravel beach popular for sunning and swimming. Another swimming beach is at Sandy Point, which is also reputed to be a fine spot for fishing.

For daytime sightseeing, **Lake Mead Cruises** (702/293-6180) leave daily on a one-and-three-quarters-hour round-trip between

Hoover Dam and Lake Mead Resort Marina. The price is $19 for adults; $9 for children ages two to eleven. Two-for-one tour coupons and other coupons for discounted fares are frequently available in the free weekly and monthly entertainment magazines.

River raft trips down the Colorado begin near the foot of Hoover Dam and end twelve miles downriver from February to November. The cost (which includes lunch) is $64.95 for adults ($79.95 includes pick-up and return to Las Vegas hotels); $35 for children five to twelve; no charge for children under the age of five.

Rockin' and Rollin' on the River

Laughlin, a town that's less than forty years old and known for a strip of gambling halls stretching along the Colorado River, doesn't seem at first glance like a promising place to bring the family. In fact, it's known as an RV-ing retirees' retreat in winter, since so many seniors take advantage of its free parking, low-cost food, and reasonably priced hotel rooms.

In summer, however, after the snowbirds have gone home, the area is a favorite with families. There's boating, fishing, and swimming on the river (**Harrah's Casino Hotel Laughlin** even has a sand beach for guests). It's a down-home sort of place, a definite contrast from Las Vegas, which is only ninety-three miles away.

Laughlin hotel/casino rooms rates generally fluctuate between $40 and $90, depending on availability and days of the week. At the times when resorts launch room-rate wars to keep occupancy levels up, rates have been known to dip as low as $9.

It's a great place for families whose teenagers can't ever seem to get enough to eat, since Laughlin's buffets have the reputation of being better and less expensive than those in Las Vegas. Breakfast buffets at Laughlin's hotel/ casinos cost from $2.99 to $3.99; lunch, from $3.99 to $5.99; dinner, from $5.99 to $8.99.

The main attractions at **Harrah's Laughlin** buffet breakfasts and brunches (702/298-4600) are the made-to-order omelets; you can order them with ham and cheese, with chorizo, black olives, onions, celery, and green pepper—or all of the above. At the **Ramada Express' Round House Buffet** (702/298-4200) a lunchtime deli provides a sandwich, soup, and salad bar where you can combine as many and as much of the ingredients into an enormous lunch.

A carving station with barons of beef and Virginia baked ham is the big draw at the **Edgewater** (702/298-2453) dinner buffet. Restaurant meals are inexpensive, too. For example, a dinner of all-you-can-eat pork, beef, and chicken ribs costs $8.95 at the **Colorado Belle** (702/298-4000).

Each year the number of Laughlin attractions increases. Among the newest is **Big Bend** of the Colorado State Recreation Area, the entrance to which is at the intersection of Casino Drive and the Needles Highway (702/298-1859). Several hundred acres of the 2,342-acre park are riverside habitat adjacent to Laughlin's southern boundary, while the remainder of the park is in the steep, rocky terrain of the Newberry Mountains. The entrance fee is $3 per car, and there's an additional $5 charge for use of the boat ramp. Park features include a beachfront picnic area with eight ramadas, a two-acre boat launch lagoon, and a sixty-foot dock.

Among the fifty stores and restaurants in **Horizon Outlet Center** (across Casino Row from the Flamingo Hilton–Laughlin; 702/298- 5111) are Guess Clothing and Guess Classics, Big Dog Sportswear, Polo, Tommy Hilfiger,

Reebok, Levi's, and Carter's Children's Wear. A 1,200-car parking garage is located in the basement of the discount shopping center, which opened in mid-1996.

Although the **Emerald River Golf Course** (1155 W. Casino Drive; 702/298-4653) is the only course in Laughlin, two more courses can be found across the river in Bullhead City, Arizona. **Chaparral Country Club** (1260 Mojave Drive; 520/758-3939) and **Riverview Golf Club** (2000 Ramar Road; 520/763-1818) are both substantially less expensive than Emerald River. Play miniature golf at the **Flamingo Hilton Laughlin** complex (1900 Casino Drive; 800/FLAMING or 702/298-5111).

Other Laughlin diversions include a riverside promenade, a six-plex movie theater, and more than seventy vintage vehicles on display at **Don Laughlin's Riverside Resort & Casino Classic Car Collection** (1650 Casino Drive; 800/227-3849 or 702/298-2535).

Several casinos operate sightseeing boats that cruise the river. Cruises cost from $10.00 to $12.95 for adults; $6.00 to $7.95 for children twelve years of age and under. Although not all the scenery along the route is exciting, the approximately ninety-minute cruises can be a pleasant diversion on warm days.

Personal watercraft may be rented at **Harrah's Casino Hotel Laughlin** (2900 S. Casino Drive; 800/HARRAHS or 702/298-4600), at New Horizons located in the **Pioneer Hotel & Gambling Hall** (2200 S. Casino Drive; 800/634-3469 or 702/298-2442), and at **Avi,** the Native-American hotel/casino located twelve miles south of Laughlin (800/284-2946 or 702/535-5555).

One of the community's biggest annual events is the **Laughlin Stampede Rodeo.** Held in early April, the Professional Rodeo Cowboys of America–sanctioned rodeo attracts top cowboys from around the country and is held in a 6,000-seat arena on the northwest corner of Edison Way and Big Bend Drive.

Another annual event of interest to families, the **Aqua Moto** Races (late May/early June) features watercraft racing on the river in front of the casinos. And on the night of July 4, the fireworks over the water with the casinos as a backdrop are spectacular (the best views are from the Arizona side of the river).

Half an hour southeast of Laughlin, historic **Oatman, Arizona,** is an authentic Old West gold mining town where wild burros still roam the streets. More than thirty arts and crafts shops, live gunfight shows, and special events are among the town's attractions.

To reach Laughlin, take the Boulder Highway (U.S. 95), being careful not to miss the turn at Railroad Pass where Highway 93 splits off from Highway 95. Turn left on Highway 163 to Laughlin. For a more scenic (and time-consuming) route, turn off Highway 95 just south of Searchlight and travel the dirt road through Christmas Tree pass, where during the holidays, pinon pine trees are decorated with some rather unusual ornaments. This is "don't forget your camera country," with spectacular granite outcroppings and giant boulders stacked on top of one another.

Although there are a few attractions at other southern Nevada border towns—Mesquite, and Primm/Stateline—they are primarily adult-oriented casino activities. Exceptions are a carousel and ferris wheel on the grounds of the **Primadonna Resort & Casino** (I-15 South; 702/382-1212) at Primm/Stateline (about half an hour from Las Vegas on the Nevada-California border) and what is billed as the world's steepest, fastest roller coaster at **Buffalo Bill's Hotel and Casino** (Stateline; 702/382-1111).

Lake Mojave

Two miles upriver from Laughlin, **Lake Mojave** is the area's outstanding attraction for nature lovers, fishermen, and water sports enthusiasts. With a shoreline of more than 150 miles, Mojave, part of the Lake Mead National Recreation Area, is a regular rest stop for migrating waterfowl and shore birds. It's also home to bald eagles, peregrine falcons, and small perching birds. Coyote, kit fox, desert bighorn sheep, roadrunners, feral burros, and horses also live in the area.

Fishermen can use all sorts of lures, live bait, and flies in their pursuit of striped and largemouth bass, catfish and crappies, trout and other species of fish that swim in the lake. To fish Lake Mojave, adults need either a valid Nevada or Arizona fishing license as well as a special use stamp. Rainbow trout fishermen must also purchase a trout stamp. No licenses or permits are required for fishermen of fourteen years and younger.

Archaeologists can't agree as to when man first inhabited the Mojave desert. There's speculation that it could have been as early as 8,000 B.C., though scientific dating techniques have only confirmed that there was human habitation in the area around 5,000 or 4,000 B.C. Petroglyphs (incised rock drawings) and pictographs (drawings on the rocks' surfaces) of the ancient people who lived in the area have survived, as have articles used by later groups of Indians who lived in the area.

The Colorado River Historical Society Museum in Bullhead City, Arizona (just north of the Laughlin Bridge; 520/754-3399) showcases ancient fossils and artifacts pertaining to the area's mining history. Nearby at the Landing are sandy beaches, boat, and personal watercraft rentals. Personal watercraft hourly rentals cost $50 for three-seaters. Fishing boats rent for $75 per day, ski boats for $250 per day.

At **Katherine's Landing** (520/754-3272), rangers lead tours and give talks about the area. Among the most popular tours are those to the Grapevine Canyon petroglyphs, seven miles west of Davis Dam, and the wildflower walks.

Digger's Delight

Some 140 years or so ago, prospectors began tramping around Nevada Territory looking for gold, silver, and other minerals to make them rich. In the years that followed, hundreds of mining camps sprang up, several of them in the area around Las Vegas. In the mountains twenty-nine miles southwest is **Potosi,** the state's oldest lode mine. **Goodsprings,** thirty-five miles southwest of Las Vegas, was a booming mining camp that produced lead and zinc at the turn of the century. Now it's a happy hunting ground for rockhounds. Other mining camps include **Sandy,** thirteen miles west of Goodsprings, and **Eldorado Canyon,** forty miles southwest of Las Vegas.

Poking around old mining camps isn't for everyone and can be downright dangerous if you don't use good sense and stay away from abandoned mine shafts and posted areas. But it is great fun if you're like a lot of Nevadans who enjoy searching for buried treasure in the form of old bottles and other artifacts of bygone days (it has been reported that digging around old outhouse sites is particularly productive since that's where people threw things they no longer wanted).

Utah's Ooh and Aah Land

Zion National Park is 159 miles northeast of Las Vegas, a drive of about three hours, since most of it is on I-15 North with its 65-mph speed limit. The Hurricane-Zion turnoff leads to Highway 9 and the park's south entrance.

The major rock formations in Zion, twenty miles south of Cedar City, Utah, have an ecclesiastical ring to their names—Great White Throne, Angels Landing, Cathedral Mountain, and

The Pulpit. And luckily for nonhikers, they're all easily seen from the roadside.

The sheer rock walls of Main Canyon have been carved by the Virgin River's constant erosion. The park's main road follows the riverbed and passes near or tunnels through some of the most brilliantly colored formations in the world. Wildlife in the park is largely of the desert variety, and most of the animals are nocturnal.

Zion's main visitor center, located at the south entrance (435/772-3256), is open daily from 8:00 A.M. to 5:00 P.M. except on Christmas and New Year's. Slide programs and exhibits detail the park's history, and you'll also find an excellent array of books in the center's bookstore. Zion Lodge is the major supplier of overnight accommodations (435/772-3213), and is also the place to go for tram tours and horseback riding in the summer season.

Garfield County's Collection of Wonders

It only takes about four hours' driving time to get from Las Vegas to **Garfield County, Utah,** and some of the most spectacular scenery in the world—scenery that inspires the imagination. Over the years its rugged territory has attracted outlaws looking for a place to hide; free spirits who want to get away from the rest of the world; pioneers; and adventurers—the stuff great stories are made of.

Best known of Utah's national parks is Bryce Canyon, a geologic fantasy of sandstone pinnacles, turrets, and spires shading from salmon pink to burnt sienna. Lined up in rows, these "hoodoos" as they're called, have been shaped by erosion, rain, wind, and frost into one of the most spectacular sights on the North American continent. Storytelling Paiutes, who lived in the region when Euro-Americans first arrived in southern Utah, explained the colorful hoodoos as "legend people" who had been turned to stone by the mythological prankster Coyote.

Fifty miles of hiking trails—twenty-three different trails in all, from the one-and-a-half-mile Queen's Garden Trail to the twenty-two-mile-long Under the Rim Trail—wind their way up, down, and along the canyon. Optimistically rated in difficulty from moderate to strenuous, none of them, in truth, are for the faint of heart—or short of breath—since the park's altitude ranges from six thousand to nine thousand feet.

You can take guided rides on horseback to the canyon floor along trails with names like Peek-A-Boo Loop and Fairyland Trail. From that vantage point, it's much easier to pick out individual formations—the Poodle, the Sunken Ship, Thor's Hammer, Queen's Garden—than it is from above. You'll also see wildflowers like gentians, yarrow, and sego lily, which because of the elevation bloom in late summer rather than early spring.

Many of the stories told by old-timers who live around Bryce are cautionary tales, to be taken seriously by hikers. They tell of people stepping too close to the canyon's rim; of campers who failed to heed warnings and got caught in flash floods.

Most colorful of the county's natural wonderlands is **Kodachrome State Park** (Visitors Center; 435/679-8562), seven miles south of Cannonville and only a short drive from Bryce. Formations at Kodachrome, which include petrified geysers, contain more iron than those at Bryce Canyon, painting them a deeper shade of red that contrasts even more handsomely with the greens of the pine, quaking aspen, and cottonwood trees.

Unlike the spires at Bryce, Kodachrome's hoodoos stand apart from one another, which has led storytellers to treat them individually and give most of them names. Like clouds, rock formations don't evoke the same images to everyone who sees them. Queen Victoria to one viewer is

Cinderella's fairy godmother to another; one person's giant cinnamon sticks may be someone else's organ pipes.

Major formations at Kodachrome, however, look undeniably like the characters and objects for which they were named—Fred Flintstone, Ballerina Slipper, Upside-Down Ice Cream Cone. Unfortunately, one of the most interesting formations, Sherlock Holmes, lost his pipe—and thus his distinctive appearance—in a 1991 earthquake.

Other stand-out attractions in the area include the five-and-a-half-mile round-trip hike to Lower Calf Creek Falls, where the waters cascade 120 feet down from the sheer canyon wall; and Anasazi Indian Village State Park, an active archaeological site with an interpretive trail and recreation of an Anasazi dwelling/storehouse.

Capitol Reef National Park (435/425-3791), with its winding canyons, nooks, and crannies, was a favorite hideout of Butch Cassidy, a Mormon boy gone bad. Now it's a hiker's paradise, with trails that explore Waterpocket Fold, a one hundred-mile-long bulge in the earth's crust containing rock pockets that catch thousands of gallons of water each year. Other trails lead to arches, windows, and canyons, as well as to the dome that is said to resemble the one on our nation's capitol.

Cedar Breaks National Monument, though resembling Bryce Canyon in appearance, is even more colorful, with ribbons of lavender, purple, and creamy gold threaded through its pink-hued formations. At **Escalante Petrified Forest State Park** (435/826-4466), two established trails lead through vast deposits of fossilized dinosaur bones and of petrified wood dating back 160 million years. And though only a small portion of Canyonlands National Park lies within Garfield County, it's a pretty spectacular portion.

If you stay overnight in Garfield County—and unless you take one of the airplane tours, you probably will—

you'll have several choices as to where to stay. The **Ruby Inn** (435/834-5341) at Bryce is the largest lodging place, but there are several area motels as well.

Arizona's Grandest Canyon

Grand Canyon—the greatest natural wonder of the world—is a destination in itself, true. But if you have only a day or two to see it in, you can do that, too. The South Rim, where most visitors go, is three hundred miles southeast of Las Vegas. That makes it only forty minutes away by air, and several airlines offer regularly scheduled air tours. They range from flights that include flyovers of the western part of the canyon with prices as low as $79 per person to overnights in luxury accommodations with lots of extras for approximately $280 ($250 for children). There are several other tours as well with various prices. Call the Tourist Center (520/638-2626).

If you decide to drive to the South Rim, plan on about five and a half hours each way. Motorcoach tours to the West Rim take about ten and a half and include such features as historical tours at the Hualapai Indian reservation and barbecue lunch overlooking the canyon (from $100 and up, depending on tour amenities).

There are still more places you might travel to from Las Vegas. **Death Valley National Monument** (760/786-2331), the country's most famous desert, is only 136 miles away, in eastern California. **Yosemite National Park** (209/372-0200) is a four-hour trip by car, and **Lake Havasu City, Arizona** (520/453-3444), where the same London Bridge that spanned the River Thames for 145 years now stands next to an English Village shopping complex (520/855-5655), is 160 miles to the southwest.

Going Commercial

Commercial sightseeing tours fit some families' travel styles, especially families whose adults like to leave the driving to someone else. Fortunately for them, there are tour operators galore in Las Vegas.

Tours to Hoover Dam, which include drive-bys of the Strip and stars' homes, and a visit to the Ethel M Chocolate Factory, cost approximately $20 for adults. Red Rock Canyon and Valley of Fire tours cost about $30 when lunch is included. Most ten- to twelve-hour motorcoach tours to Death Valley cost between $100 and $200 and those to Bryce Canyon from $90 to $130. Children's tickets are generally 5 to 15 percent less than those of adults.

It's important when you arrange for a tour to find out just what the ticket price includes—hotel pickup and return, meals, admissions, taxes, and so forth. If you have discount coupons, be sure to present them at the time you make tour arrangements.

As convenient as organized tours may be, traveling on their own by car will suit most families better, especially those with young children. Without a whole host of fellow travelers, it's possible to stop whenever someone needs—or wants—to. You'll be able to eliminate those stops the tour companies are paid to make by owners of various businesses and concessions. Best of all, you'll have the freedom to expand your stay when you're having a wonderful time and effect the sort of itinerary changes that make good trips even better.

Some Words of Caution

Whenever you go on any extended hikes at Red Rock Canyon, Valley of Fire, the Utah canyons, or any other semiwilderness area, it's important to let someone, such as a park ranger, know where you're going. Always carry water. Since temperatures plummet at higher elevations after the sun goes down, consider carrying along a windbreaker, too. And remember that rattlesnakes, scorpions, and Gila monsters make their home in various parts of the southwest, so watch where you walk and what you touch, especially when you're in rocky places or sandstone areas with crevices.

Don't forget to bring along plenty of water, either, when you're exploring the desert. Another desert hazard is flash flooding, so never attempt to drive across roadways that are covered with water of uncertain depth.

CHAPTER 11

For More Information

The Las Vegas scene is constantly expanding and changing. New businesses spring up. Hotel/casinos go from the drawing board to construction. Restaurants open, and sometimes close.

Fortunately, several sources of information remain constant. These are the sources you should contact while you're planning your trip or after you arrive in town. If they don't have what you're looking for, they'll most likely lead you to other sources that do.

Vacation Plan

The more information you have, the easier trip planning becomes. Free publications include:

CityLife (weekly)
1385 Pama Lane, No. 111
Las Vegas, NV 89119
702/871-6780

The Insider Viewpoint of Las Vegas (monthly)
9030 W. Sahara Avenue, Suite 423
Las Vegas, NV 89117
702/242-4482

Showbiz Magazine (weekly)
Las Vegas Sun
2290 Corporate Circle, No. 250
Henderson, NV 89014
702/383-7185

Today in Las Vegas (weekly)
3626 Pecos McLeod, Suite 14
Las Vegas, NV 89121
702/385-2737

Tourguide (weekly)
4440 S. Arville Street, Suite 12
Las Vegas, NV 89103
702/221-5000

Vegas Visitor (weekly)
3110 Polaris Avenue, No. 27
Las Vegas, NV 89116
702/257-8053

What's on in Las Vegas (bi-weekly, among most informative)
4425 S. Industrial Road
Las Vegas, NV 89103
702/891-8811

Where
500 S. Rancho Drive, Suite 7
Las Vegas, NV 89106
702/258-8585

Most of these magazines are 5 by 8 inches or tabloid size. Although the majority of them are available on a yearly subscription basis, prices are very high—it's not uncommon for this type of publication to cost $75 to $100 when sent through the mail. However, many of the publications are happy to send a free sample copy. One publication that could be worth subscribing to if you're interested in bargains—though it's heavy on those associated with gaming—is *Las Vegas Advisor* (3687 S. Procyon Avenue, Las Vegas, NV 89103; 702/252-0655). Subscription price for the monthly twelve-page newsletter is $45 a year/$5 a single copy.

You'll find these magazines all over town after you arrive. Since they are helpful for advance planning, however, when you aren't able to get them directly from their publishers, you might want to request copies from the Las Vegas Convention & Visitors Authority (LVCVA) tourism department or the Las Vegas Chamber of Commerce. Their addresses and phone numbers are:

Las Vegas Convention & Visitors Authority
3150 Paradise Road
Las Vegas, NV 89109
702/892-0711

Las Vegas Chamber of Commerce
3720 Howard Hughes Parkway, No. 100
Las Vegas, NV 89109
702/735-1616

You can also obtain a wealth of brochures, freebie/discount coupons, an occasional funbook, maps of Las Vegas, and information on various areas of interest by writing these organizations.

Discount coupons are especially important for families on a tight vacation budget. They're great money stretchers when you want to visit an attraction, eat at a restaurant, stay at a hotel, or take a tour and can match up discount coupons with those attractions or businesses.

In-flight magazines of airlines serving Las Vegas often have ads containing freebie or discount coupons, too. Coupons that give discounts on auto rentals can be particularly helpful. Prior to your trip, obtain copies of in-flight magazines of airlines that fly to Las Vegas (flying with a particular airline isn't a requirement for use of coupons found in their magazines). Southwest Airline's and Reno Air's in-flights are particularly good coupon sources.

Four tourist centers on the Strip provide information on attractions and tours as well as brochures and free/discount coupons. The centers are clearly marked, so you shouldn't have any trouble finding them. You'll find the weekly magazines at Traveler's Aid and the Bell Trans desk on the baggage level at McCarran International Airport; in all the major hotels (usually at the bell or concierge desks); at the Greyhound bus depot downtown; at the tourism office at the Las Vegas Convention Center; and in the racks at the Las Vegas Chamber of Commerce.

Three other chambers of commerce that will be able to give you information are:

Asian Chamber of Commerce
900 Karen Avenue, Suite C217
Las Vegas, NV 89109
702/737-4300

Nevada Black Chamber of Commerce
1048 W. Owens Avenue
Las Vegas, NV 89106
702/648-6222

Latin Chamber of Commerce
829 S. Sixth Street, No. 3

Las Vegas, NV 89101
702/385-7367

Other prominent ethnic organizations include the Filipino
American Federation of Nevada, Inc., Thailand Nevada Associ-
ation, Japanese American Club of Las Vegas, Las Vegas Korean
Association, and Las Vegas Hawaiian Civic Club. Since their con-
tact people change with the clubs' annual elections, it's best to
get the organizations' names and telephone numbers from the
Las Vegas Convention and Visitors Authority or the Las Vegas
Chamber of Commerce.

A publication that's especially useful for visitors interested in
ethnic businesses and special events is the *Official Ethnic Guide*,
published semi-annually and available through the Las Vegas
Convention & Visitors Authority.

One of the very best resources for general information that's
available after you arrive in Las Vegas is the *Sprint Yellow Pages
Telephone Directory*. In addition to the directory listings, it contains several pages of sectional maps of the area, diagrams of
most major non-casino entertainment venues and sports stadi-
ums, a diagram of McCarran International Airport, and hundreds of discount coupons.

Accommodations

For ratings and basic information about various Las Vegas
lodging places, your best sources are the *AAA California/Nevada
Tourbook*, available at American Automobile Association offices
(free to members; $8.75 to non-members) and the *California
and the West Mobil Travel Guide*, available at bookstores and at
most public library reference desks.

It's possible to get additional information about accommodations by asking to see any of the hotel guides used by the travel
agency you patronize. The *Star* ratings are especially good as

their evaluations of properties are extremely candid. The following hotel/casino list with their addresses and toll-free telephone numbers should be helpful in finding out about their rates and any packages they may be offering.

Hotel/Casino	Address	Toll-Free
Aladdin	3667 Las Vegas Blvd. S.	877/333-9474
Alexis Park	375 E. Harmon Ave.	800/582-2228
Arizona Charlie's	740 S. Decatur Blvd.	800/342-2695
Bally's Resort	3645 Las Vegas Blvd. S.	800/634-3434
Barbary Coast	3595 Las Vegas Blvd. S.	800/227-2279
Bellagio Resort Hotel	Las Vegas Blvd. S.	888/987-6667
Binion's Horseshoe	128 Fremont St.	800/237-6537
Boulder Station	4111 Boulder Hwy.	800/683-7777
Bourbon Street	120 E. Flamingo Rd.	800/634-6956
Caesars Palace	3570 Las Vegas Blvd. S.	800/634-6661
California Hotel	First & Ogden	800/634-6255
Castaways	2800 Fremont St.	800/826-2800
Circus Circus	2880 Las Vegas Blvd. S.	800/634-3450
Courtyard by Marriott	3275 Paradise Rd.	800/321-2211
El Cortez	600 Fremont St.	800/634-6703
Excalibur	3850 Las Vegas Blvd. S.	800/937-7777
Fiesta	2400 N. Rancho Dr.	800/731-7333
Fitzgeralds Holiday Inn	301 E. Fremont St.	800/274-5825
Flamingo Hilton	3555 Las Vegas Blvd. S.	800/732-2111

Hotel/Casino	Address	Toll-Free
Four Queens	202 E. Fremont St.	800/634-6045
Four Seasons	3960 Las Vegas Blvd. S.	877/632-5200
Fremont Hotel	200 Fremont St.	800/634-6182
Gold Coast	4000 W. Flamingo Rd.	800/402-6278
Gold Spike	400 E. Ogden	800/634-6703
Golden Gate	111 S. Main St.	800/426-1906
Golden Nugget	129 E. Fremont St.	800/634-3454
Harrah's	3475 Las Vegas Blvd. S.	800/634-6765
Holiday Inn/Boardwalk	3750 Las Vegas Blvd. S.	800/635-4581
Hotel San Remo	115 E. Tropicana Ave.	800/522-7366
Hyatt Regency Lake Las Vegas	101 Montelago Blvd.	800/223-1234
Imperial Palace	3535 Las Vegas Blvd. S.	800/634-6441
Jackie Gaughan's Plaza	1 Main Street	800-634-6575
Lady Luck	206 N. Third Street	800-523-9582
Las Vegas Club	18 E. Fremont St.	800/634-6532
Las Vegas Hilton	3000 Paradise Rd.	800/732-7117
Luxor	3900 Las Vegas Blvd. S.	800/288-1000
Main Street Station	200 N. Main St.	800/465-0711
Mandalay Bay	3950 Las Vegas Blvd. S.	877/632-7700
Maxim Hotel	160 E. Flamingo Rd.	800/634-6987
MGM Grand	3799 Las Vegas Blvd. S.	800/929-1111
Mirage	3400 Las Vegas Blvd. S.	800/627-6667

Hotel/Casino	Address	Toll-Free
Monte Carlo	3770 Las Vegas Blvd. S.	800/822-8652
Nevada Palace	5255 Boulder Hwy.	800/634-6283
New Frontier Hotel	3120 Las Vegas Blvd. S.	800/634-6966
New York-New York	3790 Las Vegas Blvd. S.	800/693-6763
Orleans	4500 W. Tropicana Ave.	800/675-3267
Palace Station	2411 W. Sahara Ave.	800/634-3101
Paris Las Vegas	3655 Las Vegas Blvd. S.	800/Bon-Jour
Plaza Suite Hotel	4255 S. Paradise Rd.	800/654-2000
Regent Las Vegas	221 N. Rampart Blvd.	800/869-7777
Reserve Hotel	777 W. Lake Mead Dr., Henderson	888/899-7770
Residence Inn by Marriott	3225 Paradise Rd.	800/331-3131
Rio Suite Hotel	3700 W. Flamingo Rd.	800/888-1808
Riviera	2901 Las Vegas Blvd. S.	800/634-6753
Royal Las Vegas	99 Convention Center Dr.	800/634-6118
Sahara	2535 Las Vegas Blvd. S.	800/696-2121
Sam's Town	511 Boulder Hwy.	800/634-6371
Santa Fe	4949 N. Rancho Dr.	800/872-6823
Silverton Hotel-Casino	3333 Blue Diamond Rd.	800/588-7711
Stardust	3000 Las Vegas Blvd. S.	800/634-6757
Stratosphere	2000 Las Vegas Blvd. S.	800/998-6937
Sunset Station	1301 W. Sunset Rd.	888/786-7389

Hotel/Casino	Address	Toll-Free
Terrible's Town Casino & Bowl	6425 Boulder Hwy.	800/640-9777
Texas Station	2101 Texas Star Ln.	800/654-8888
The Venetian	3355 Las Vegas Blvd. S.	888/283-6423
Treasure Island	3300 Las Vegas Blvd. S.	800/944-7444
Tropicana	3801 Las Vegas Blvd. S.	800/634-4000
Vacation Village	6711 Las Vegas Blvd. S.	800/338-0608
Westward Ho	2900 Las Vegas Blvd. S.	800/634- 6803

Since most of the Las Vegas hotel/casinos have been built within the past thirty years—and a good share of the top properties within the past ten—you can expect fairly large rooms, whatever the price. Also, almost all hotels have smoke alarms and automatic sprinkler systems that activate in case of fire.

The most conveniently located hostel is:

Las Vegas International Hostel
1208 Las Vegas Boulevard S.
702/385-9955

Travelers with disabilities may want to contact Nevada Association for the Handicapped (6200 West Oakey Boulevard, Las Vegas, NV 89102; 702/870-7050) and Southern Nevada Sightless (1001 North Bruce Street, Las Vegas, NV 89101; 702/642-0100) for information on accommodations in Las Vegas, although most major properties have rooms that are especially designed and equipped for the disabled.

Transportation

If you're driving to Las Vegas, you'll want the official Nevada state map. You can get one from the Nevada State Commission on Tourism, Capitol Complex, Carson City, NV 89710-0005; 800/NEVADA-8 or 775/687-3636.

Drivers will be ahead of the game by obtaining a good map of Las Vegas and studying it in advance. Having a general idea of which streets run in what directions can save time and tempers. "Streetwise Las Vegas" ($5.95, available at major bookstores) is one of the best and folds into a convenient 3^3 /₄by-8^1 /₂inch rectangle. Other good maps, which you can also buy at bookstores, are B & B City Streets ($6.95) and Rand McNally ($5.95).

Copies of Citizen's Area Transit (CAT) system's "Transportation Center System Map and Guide to Services" and "Time Schedule and Map Book" are in racks at the entrances to all CAT buses and at the Downtown Transportation Center (DTC), 300 N. Casino Center Boulevard.

They can also be obtained by contacting:

Regional Transportation Commission of Clark County
301 E. Clark Avenue, Suite 300
Las Vegas, NV 89101
702/228-7433

Dining

There's no single source of objective dining information for the Las Vegas area, so the best way to determine whether you want to eat in a particular restaurant is to (1) look it over, and (2) ask to see a copy of the menu. Restaurant write-ups in the weekly publications are almost always about places that advertise in those publications.

For more unbiased appraisals, check out back issues of

Nevada Magazine for in-depth reviews that are listed in the publication's table of contents. Restaurants are also reviewed in the local newspapers. You'll find these back issues in the Periodicals section of the Las Vegas Library at 833 Las Vegas Boulevard N.; 702/382-3493.

Attractions, Events, Activities, and Entertainment

Buying the issue of *Nevada Magazine* that's on the newsstands while you're in town is also an excellent way to find out what's going on in town—from special exhibits at art galleries and craft shows to chili cook-offs and symphony orchestra concerts. If you want to subscribe to the magazine, which is published every two months ($16.95 per year, $22.95, foreign), the address is:

Nevada Magazine
401 N. Carson Street, Suite 100
Carson City, NV 89710-4291
775/687-5416

In addition to the free weekly/bi-weekly, and monthly magazines listed above, you'll get valuable information by reading the newspapers. The major daily newspaper is:

Las Vegas Review Journal
P.O. Box 70
Las Vegas, NV 89125
702/383-0400

The Friday and Saturday editions of the *Las Vegas Review Journal* are especially useful, since in addition to information they also contain excellent discount coupons, such as two-for-one admissions to King Arthur's Tournament at Excalibur.

For information on specific activities and attractions, you may want to contact the following.

Las Vegas Parks and Recreation Department
2601 East Sunset Road
Las Vegas, Nevada 89120
702/455-8200

The people at the recreation department are extremely helpful and can provide you with information about activities, parks, and recreational facilities such as exercise courses, swimming pools, and picnic areas. If they don't have the answers to your questions, they'll tell you where to find them.

Especially for Kids

You might want to watch community affairs announcements on KLAS TV, Channel 8, weekdays between 8:00 A.M. and 8:30 A.M. for organization-sponsored events geared to families, such as ethnic festivals and school carnivals.

Day Trips and Excursions

To be sure you don't miss a thing on your day trips and excursions, get advance information on what to do and see. The following addresses and phone numbers are good ones to contact:

Nevada State Parks:	**Nevada Division of State Parks** Capitol Complex Carson City, NV 89710 775/687-4384
Mt. Charleston:	**U.S. Department of the Interior** 550 East Charleston Las Vegas, NV 89104

702/873-8800

Red Rock Canyon trails:	**Bureau of Land Management** Las Vegas District Office P.O. Box 26569 Las Vegas, NV 89126 702/647-5000

Valley of Fire: **Valley of Fire State Park**
Box 515
Overton, NV 89040
702/397-2088

Lake Mead: **National Park Service**
Lake Mead National Recreation
  Area
601 Nevada Highway
Boulder City, NV 89005
702/293-8907

(The park service will be able to give you information on such things as camp sites, and numbers you can call to find out about scuba gear, scuba classes, houseboat rentals, and other Lake Mead activities.)

Laughlin area: **Laughlin Visitor Center**
1555 Casino Drive, Box 502
Laughlin, NV 89029
702/298-3321

Hunting and Fishing: **Nevada Division of Wildlife**
State Mall Complex
Las Vegas, NV 89158

702/486-5127

Out-of-State Sources: **Arizona Office of Tourism**
2702 N. 3rd Street, No. 4015
Phoenix, AZ 85007
602/230-7733

**Grand Canyon National Park
  Lodges**
1 Main Street
Grand Canyon, AZ 86023
520/638-2631

Sierra Club
812 N. 3rd Street
Phoenix, AZ 85004
602/253-8633

Dixie National Forest
Powell Ranger District
P.O. Box 80
Panguitch, UT 84759
435/676-8815

Garfield County Travel Council
P.O. Box 200
Panguitch, UT 84759
800/444-6689

**Iron County Tourism and
  Convention Bureau**
286 N. Main
Cedar City, UT 84720

801/586-5124

**Utah Division of Parks and
    Recreation**
1594 W. North Temple, Suite 116
Salt Lake City, UT 84116
801/538-7220

Zion National Park
Springdale, UT 84767-1099
435/772-3256

Commerical Tours: **Adventure Photo Tours**
702/889-8687

**Eagle Canyon & Scenic Airlines
    Grand Canyon Tours**
702/736-3333

**Golden West Land & Cattle
    Corp.**
(horseback)
702/798-7788

Gray Line Tours
702/384-1234

Las Vegas Tour and Travel
702/739-8975

Rebel Adventure Tours
702/380-6969

A great deal of information about all the destinations mentioned in the Excursions chapter is available on the Internet. Search engines Google and Yahoo are especially effective in providing multiple information sources. Among the especially useful Web sites you can find are:

www.americanparknetwork.com
www.death.valley.national-park.com/hike.htm
www.desertusa.com
www.infowest.com
www.nps.gov
www.thecanyon.com
www.xpressweb.com/parks

There are several books on the market describing hikes in the Las Vegas area and the Utah parks. *Hiking Las Vegas* by Branch Whitney (Huntington Press, $17.95) is an excellent guide with lots of photos and maps. Sixty hikes within sixty minutes of the Las Vegas Strip are described. Information about trailhead location, length of hike, elevation gain, peak elevation, time range that hikers can expect the hike to take (up and back), difficulty of hike, and how easy the trail is to follow is given at the beginning of each section. Each hike is also assigned a danger level, which takes into account the possibility of falling, altitude sickness, and potential weather situations such as flash floods. Difficulty is divided into five classes, ranging from easy hiking to rock climbing and the author designates each hike's suitability for children (ages five to eleven) accompanied by an adult. Comments on the hike and a short description of each trail follows the practical information.

Hiking Zion and Bryce Canyon National Parks by Erik Molvar and Tamara Martin (Falcon Press, $14.95) is another gem. With abundant photos and trail diagrams, it includes fifty-six hikes and includes the same sort of material as the previous book, but is more detailed as far as description of the hikes are concerned. It also includes information on the best season to take each hike and whether water is available.

Campers will want to buy *Utah and Nevada Camping* by Gayen and Tom Wharton and Deke Castleman (Foghorn Press, $18.95). Twenty-two pages are devoted to camping facilities in the Las Vegas area, while the section on Bryce, Zion, Cathedral Gorge, and Canyonlands campgrounds is substantially larger.

If your family is interested in botany and you plan to take any treks through the desert or up Mt. Charleston, *Weeds of the West,* published by the Western Society of Weed Science in cooperation with the Western United States Land Grant Universities Cooperative Extension Services ($24.95) is a good resource—though heavy to carry along.

One last suggestion: When you can't seem to find the information you're looking for, phone the reference desk at the Las Vegas Library, 702/733-3613. The people there are skilled at research and are almost sure to be able to answer your questions.

Index

About the Author

Connie Emerson is the author of eleven books, including several volumes in Citadel Press's popular Cheapskate's Guide series (specifically, guides to Las Vegas, San Francisco, London, Paris, Rome, and Venice). She has also published twenty children's stories and more than five-hundred articles in national magazines and newspapers, including the *Los Angeles Times*, the *Christian Science Monitor*, and the *New York Post*. Her professional affiliations include membership in the Society of American Travel Writers. Residents of Nevada for more than twenty-five years, the author and her husband have two sons and two grandsons.